The Little Book of Big Ideas

Leaders in Agriculture share their Management and Leadership Insight

Compiled by Ben Woolley

Dedication

For my immediate family.

Stacey who has kept me straight for 35 years.

For my Children, David and Jessica who have brought me endless joy and pride and taught me so much about myself.

For my brothers and Sister, Giles, Robert and Lib, who toughened me up and made me who I am today.

All profits from the sale of this book will go to charity and worthwhile causes.

About the Author

Ben was born in the UK, where he lived until he was sixteen. He moved to the USA with his parents and finished school, then attended the University of Georgia, where he earned a degree in Agricultural Economics.

He worked in the family business—outdoor sow production—until his father's untimely death. He went on to establish the nursery and finisher system for Hanor in Illinois and then moved to Scotland to overhaul the production of A. Simmers Ltd., PIC's largest multiplier in Europe.

He later moved to Alberta, where he worked at Sunterra Enterprises for 25 years, retiring at the end of 2022. While there, he built the pig production to supply 450,000 antibiotic-free pigs, and a management company in the US managed a further half million pigs. He also managed the slaughter plant and sheep feedlot.

Upon retirement, Ben bought into the 21st Century Forums and founded the 21st Century Leadership Forums and the Leadership

Course. Over 150 young leaders have completed the Leadership Course at the time of writing.

Ben is married to Stacey, who graduated *magna cum laude* in Economics from Vanderbilt. They have two children, both of whom were valedictorians of their classes. (Not home-schooled, Carl!!) Both are married. David is a mechanical engineer and oversees the design department at Nortrak, and his wife, Britt, is a high-risk delivery nurse. Jessica is an accountant and Senior Manager at KPMG, and her husband is also an accountant and financial analyst for a real estate company in Calgary.

Contents

Now, When We Get There...

When I was a young boy, we used to go on vacation to a cottage my parents rented in Carno, in Wales. The house had no running water or electricity, and we had one bath a week while there—in the cattle trough, fed by a freezing cold stream running down from the hill.

Some of my fondest memories as a child were roaming the hills, moors, and streams around the cottage.

The drive from our house in Berkshire to the cottage was brutal. I think we visited every gateway at some time for one of the four children to be sick or need a pee! As the youngest, I spent most of the journey curled up on the floor of the back seat to avoid the running battle going on above me. When we got there, we children just wanted to get away from the car.

My Dad used to make a speech while driving up to the cottage that started, *"Now when we get there..."* It continued, *"...I don't want you all running off; stay and help your Mother and I carry everything in."*

The car stopped in the farmyard, the doors flew open, and four children vanished in an instant.

"Now when we get there..." means be prepared **before** you get there.

The chapters in this book are all very different. Read between the lines, and you will find nuggets from the stories and ideas of all of the contributors.

I hope you find this book useful.

Introduction

When I was in my mid-20s, my father thought it would be a good idea to enroll me in an American Management Association course on leadership and management. At the time, I already had a degree in economics from the University of Georgia. However, what I learned during that course proved to be as valuable as all the classes I had taken at university.

The course gave me a structured approach to effectively managing and motivating both teams and individual employees. It sparked a lifelong passion for learning about leadership. Since then, I've read many books on the subject, as well as on related topics that piqued my interest.

When I retired at the end of 2023 from Sunterra and became more involved with the 21st Century, we decided to launch a leadership course tailored for young people beginning their journey into leadership roles in agriculture. The course has been a success. At the time of writing, we've guided more than 150 young leaders through the two-year program. We are also preparing to launch two additional courses: one for farm managers and another for executives, allowing them to continue their learning journey.

Young people need to understand that there is a structured, effective way to lead and manage people. There truly is a right way and a wrong way. Without learning the right approach, many will struggle to reach their full potential or become successful leaders.

Interestingly, I've also learned a lot from the participants in our leadership course. One key insight is the importance of young people learning from those who have held leadership roles for many years—gaining wisdom from both their successes and their failures.

This realization led me to reflect on how much valuable knowledge is lost when leaders retire without sharing what they've learned with the next generation.

So, I decided to reach out to some of the best leaders I know and ask if they'd be willing to contribute insights to a book—so that their wisdom wouldn't be lost but preserved and passed on.

I also invited our two leadership consultants, Shonda Sammons and Kristen Cumming, to add their thoughts. Shonda offers her perspective on why formal leadership training is so important, while Kristen shares common leadership mistakes she's encountered in her consulting work.

I cannot express how grateful I am to everyone who agreed to contribute to this book. These are busy individuals, and each one dedicated significant time and thought to writing their chapter.

Their willingness to do so shows that they, too, recognize the importance of passing on their knowledge.

All profits from the book will be donated to a selection of chosen charities.

This project is a genuine effort to pass on insights that will help the next generation of leaders become more effective in working with their teams. If just one reader finds a meaningful nugget that helps them become a better leader, then the effort will have been worthwhile.

I hope you enjoy reading the chapters as much as I did.

– Ben Woolley

Chapter 1: Common Mistakes in Leadership

Kristen Cumming

Kristen Cumming is my Business Partner and a brilliant Leadership and Management Consultant. I am very lucky to get to work with her.

Kristen lives in Edmonton, Alberta.

"Let these be a lesson to you...cautionary tales about leading and leadership."

- **Kristen Cumming**

Over 25 years assessing, coaching, and training leaders across all sectors, there are a few common mistakes I've seen. These mistakes may illustrate some important principles of leadership that we can all learn from—and ideally use to improve our own practice.

You don't know what you're here to do.

The leader's job is to mobilize people toward agreed-upon, desired outcomes. The outcomes represent a preferred future state—a vision, of sorts. A vision isn't just useful at the enterprise level. Every team has value to the enterprise that they can strive to improve; therefore, every team can have a vision. Sometimes, the leader either doesn't know or doesn't communicate that vision. This has very predictable effects on teams: it creates complacency, chaotic busyness, and conflict within and between teams.

Let's look at complacency first. Imagine a time when you had to overcome some challenge or discomfort. Many people have taken on a home renovation or similar project that came with its fair share of frustration. Imagine living through that project—with all the mess and uncertainty—without a picture in your mind of the end result. This is, unfortunately, how many people exist at work. They endure the mess and uncertainty, day in and day out, without a picture of success in their mind to motivate them and give them purpose—without a clear reason to try. Without that vision, people lose a sense of meaning in their work. Their work ceases to matter to any greater outcome. They can't measure progress and may feel that they just drone away on an endless treadmill. This often results in complacency and ends with people doing just enough to get by.

When the leader doesn't have a strong sense of the vision or purpose of the team, another possible result is chaotic busyness. A team's clarity of purpose determines how they best add value to the organization and helps them understand how they should use their time and resources. Leaders should know clearly and confidently which choices create value and which do not. Do not assume that the leader is the only person making choices. Everyone in an organization makes choices—at all levels—that can create more or less value. When the leader is clear, their teams then know how to align their individual decisions. Without that clarity, leaders end up saying yes to things outside of their best purpose and stretch people and resources thin in ways that don't bring the greatest value to the company. We've likely all seen examples of this: where teams are running ragged but producing little value. They seem busy—there is a lot of activity—but on closer examination, there is little impact or value creation.

Without a clear understanding of purpose and desired results, people can often end up in conflict. When the leader doesn't establish a clear vision, people will work toward their own versions of success that may be at cross-purposes with each other. This can create territorialism and defensive behaviours. If people don't know how their work matters to organizational outcomes, they may feel vulnerable and unvalued. The combination of defensiveness, vulnerability, and uncertainty is the perfect breeding ground for team dysfunction and unhealthy conflict.

The lesson: watch your team for a moment from an objective perspective, and ask yourself: do I have clarity about our purpose and contributions to organizational outcomes? Have I shared that purpose clearly and frequently with teams and individuals? Have I communicated progress and celebrated successes?

Every team, every individual, deserves a purpose—and will perform better for having it. The humblest roles often have the greatest impact on a company's success. Take time to get crystal clear about that impact for yourself as a leader and communicate it clearly and frequently. Get real indicators of progress and celebrate success. Then, watch your team again and note any changes you may see.

Good enough isn't good enough for long

The next mistake I've observed is leaders who do not invest in skills development—either for themselves or their teams. It is, unfortunately, all too common. People are busy, teams are understaffed, and it is never convenient to pause for learning. Years can slip by without investing in developing talent, and this can be deceivingly tolerable for many companies. People are generally skilled enough to do the job, and holding training for the sake of training may not make sense. The problem is that investing in talent development serves more needs than just training. It signals value for the employee, gets people thinking outside of their current context, and proactively enables them to weather change.

One of the most troubling patterns I've observed is when companies invest in training to correct problematic behaviour. When there is a case of harassment, the company invests in respectful workplace training. When there is a case of theft, the company replays the ethics video for the fifth time. Imagine how a high-performing employee may perceive this pattern. When we use training primarily as a corrective effort, we consume the budget we could direct into great development investments in employees who want to perform, learn, and grow with the company. Investing in talent can be a way of recognizing performance and potential. Without it, high-performing employees may feel disengaged or taken for granted; they may languish.

Another trouble zone is when an organization has a stable team of employees who are not learning and, therefore, fall into a routine that can become complacent. Whether or not employees have to learn something for the job today, they just need to be learning. When we are learning, we flex the mental muscles that allow us to see problems from a new angle and to consider solutions we hadn't previously imagined. Learning is about exploring what we don't already know, and the more frequently and comfortably we go there, the more we can think outside of our current context. This can have tremendous value to organizations—imagine a more innovative workforce with more perspectives to draw upon when facing challenges.

Learning is also a great rehearsal for change. If you keep the team learning, you keep the team better prepared for change. A team that frequently engages in learning new ideas, perspectives, or techniques will be more adaptive to change and uncertainty. Learning is about navigating what we don't know, and change is much the same. Finally, leadership and learning are very connected. A leader must be a learner to retain their ability to explore possibilities, connect with new ideas, and prepare themselves for change ahead. *Don't forget to invest in yourself!*

The lesson: remember that learning can happen in many ways—not all of which are in a traditional classroom. Teams may listen to a podcast together and take a few minutes to discuss what they heard. You may bring training into the organization when you want consistent messaging and group uptake. You may send individuals to training, conferences, or industry events when you want to bring in multiple outside perspectives. Don't forget yourself! A leader who isn't learning isn't building their ability to lead.

I can't trust your yes if you never say no.

The third and most common mistake I see is when leaders don't say no or challenge the status quo. This has a number of consequences, which include poor decisions, lost resources, and a breakdown of trust.

It can feel incredibly risky to speak up at work, particularly if you perceive that you are the only person who holds a different view than others. I think everyone can recall a time when they felt uncertain about asking a question or sharing an alternate perspective—especially when speaking up to someone in a more senior position. We likely didn't enjoy asking a question in a classroom full of people who seemed to know the answer.

Sometimes, this looks like having the "meeting after the meeting," where we air our grievances in the safety of our closest friends but withhold those opinions when decisions are being made. Sometimes, it looks like consenting to a course of action we know won't work, rather than risk being the contrary voice. Sometimes, it means withholding feedback from someone who may help them rather than risking discomfort. Speaking up often feels very lonely, and being singled out like that makes us feel vulnerable to social rejection. Sometimes, it feels much safer to follow the crowd.

Unfortunately, leadership is rarely comfortable, and the leader's job is not to follow the crowd. The leader's job is to take a position in service to the organization and the people who work there. This often means engaging in healthy, productive conflict, ensuring that perspectives are considered in decision-making and challenging authority.

When we withhold our perspectives, we unknowingly stifle others from sharing theirs. I've sat in on countless meetings in which people expressed to me privately that they disagreed with a direction yet did not speak up in front of the group. We wrongly assume that if no one speaks up, people are largely in agreement—we assume this even as we disagree and don't say it! By this logic, decisions can be passively endorsed by a group of people who largely disagree, and no one knows it. As this goes on, the organization begins to make increasingly poor choices that are not properly discussed or evaluated—until, eventually, it becomes unsustainable. This consumes organizational resources, like time and money, in ways that don't create value and leave teams chronically under-resourced. It takes individual courage, but bearing the risk of speaking up is the safest thing for the organization.

Consider how this same pattern plays out between people. Imagine I knew a way you could improve your outcomes at work, but I didn't tell you. Imagine how you would feel when you found out. On some level, we may feel a bit betrayed and vulnerable.

When we withhold useful feedback from one another, it destroys trust. When we speak up with genuine concern for each other's outcomes, it builds trust. However, to get to that trust, we have to pass through a state of discomfort. People may feel exposed, embarrassed, or anxious—as we do when we care about our work and want to be good at it. That initial response is uncomfortable, and as a result, many people avoid speaking up to one another directly and candidly. Therefore, many people exist in a chronic state of distrust, as their colleagues withhold feedback and endorse decisions and actions that they don't actually support. This begins to erode healthy conflict, effective decision-making, and collective trust.

The lesson: as a leader, normalize speaking up with your teams. Appreciate when people bring alternate views to the discussion. Invite feedback from your team. Regularly ask them, "What can I do more or less to help you or this team?" With your peers and leaders, ask them for feedback and inquire if and how they'd like to get feedback from you.

No news is not good news.

The final mistake I've seen is failing to take account of the effort of employees. So many days are spent firefighting and chasing after problems that many leaders simply run out of time and energy to say thanks and express gratitude. Unfortunately, it divides leaders and followers into an "us and them" dynamic, can cost talent and commitment, and kills clarity of purpose.

When leaders miss opportunities to take account of effort, employees may interpret that their work either isn't enough or doesn't matter. In either case, it leaves the employee uncertain whether they are doing a good job. For high performers, this can erode their ambition and cause them to seek work elsewhere. For poorer performers, it reinforces the notion that nothing will ever be good enough, so there's no point in trying.

Note that taking account of effort doesn't mean everyone gets a trophy for mediocre results. Taking account of effort means the leader notices the employee's work and provides personal, specific, timely feedback on performance that is rich with data and gives the employee clarity on how their effort creates desired results—so they can make adjustments to create greater and greater value.

Consider, too, that taking account of effort and expressing gratitude also clarifies how that employee supports organizational objectives. Through appreciation, we reinforce what matters. If you've made a company-wide commitment to safe working habits, saying a quick thanks when you see someone take an opportunity to correct a hazard takes little time, no money, and minimal effort—but can reinforce that person's clarity of purpose and commitment to organizational results.

The lesson: set aside at least 10 minutes each day to find a way to recognize effort. It may be a quick email or note, pulling someone aside on the job to say thanks, or taking someone for lunch. Sometimes, it looks like bringing a crew coffee and donuts after they complete a project or checking in with a new hire to tell them how well they're getting up to speed. Ensure that you have real indicators of values and that you clearly connect the person's effort to the value they create.

Give a little grace

Leadership is not for the faint of heart—it is challenging to align diverse people in a shared direction and impossible to get it right for everybody all the time.

Remember this old horse trainer's adage: *expect everything and accept anything.* Apply that to the people you lead and to yourself as you try to serve your organization and the people within it. Hold expectations high and provide all the clarity, development, candid feedback, and appreciation you can so that people can give their best. And be humble—give grace, both to yourself and those around you—as you figure it out together.

Chapter 2: Servant Leadership

Steve Weiss

Steve is the Founder of Nutriquest Solutions in Mason City, Iowa, a highly successful business servicing the Agriculture Industry. Steve is also a Partner in the 21st Century Forums and is an accountant by training.

Simply a Servant

Biography of the Author

Steve Weiss is the founder and CEO of NutriQuest, CEO of Hoover's Hatchery, and a partner in 21st Century Strategic Forums. He also serves as a board member for several enterprises in the U.S. swine industry and non-profit sectors.

At NutriQuest, Steve leads a team that has developed and commercialized over 30 technologies to improve livestock and poultry performance and help solve key industry challenges—such as humane euthanasia and improving bacon quality, among others. NutriQuest acquired Hoover's Hatchery in 2015 and, through growth and acquisition, transformed a regional business into the largest producer of chicks for the backyard farming industry in the U.S. Steve has also been an active and outspoken industry leader in his role with 21st Century Strategic Forums, leading efforts and dialogue around animal rights activism, antibiotic preservation, fake meat, and other industry challenges.

Steve was previously a founder and CFO at Iowa Select Farms, one of the largest and most successful swine producers in the U.S. He has also served as a turnaround specialist for several companies and as a consultant to numerous distressed production agriculture businesses—successfully accomplishing restructurings or the sale and continuity of those businesses in each case.

A Certified Public Accountant, Steve was a founding partner of Roth & Company, a Des Moines, Iowa-based CPA firm subsequently acquired by Eide Bailly. He was also Manager of Middle Market Services for Deloitte from 1985 to 1990.

The title of this chapter is not meant to attempt to describe Mr. Weiss as a leader, but rather to describe his father and mother—and what he has learned is simply the most important element of being an effective leader.

Since this chapter was written, Marie Weiss, my mother of 103 years, passed away. She died with the same dignity and grace with which she lived her 103+ years. Mom left a legacy borne of the greatest form of leadership and lifelong occupation—that of a mother of 10 children and 91 descendants.

Introduction

If I have learned one thing in my career about leadership, it's that you won't learn how to be an effective leader from a business book or a biography of a great military or political leader. Rather, you'll pick it up from all life experiences—and primarily from key role models in your life. And if you want to really be the best leader you can be, learn from the undisputed best leader of all time. The best book that I've ever read on leadership is *The Servant* by James Hunter. Its basic principles are derived from the greatest leader of all time and the oldest book of all time that captured his life and his message… inspiring countless followers of these basic principles even today, centuries later. Of course, I'm talking about Jesus Christ and the Holy Bible.

Growing up, I didn't realize it at the time, but I had the best role models that one could possibly have. My parents and grandparents were hard-working, faith-filled people who not only served as great role models but challenged me to strive to be Christ-centered. I am the ninth of ten children of Clem and Marie Weiss, which made me doubly blessed. I also benefited from each of my older siblings, and each one of them was a positive role model for me.

As I grew up and had to choose my own role models, I was blessed with such a myriad of experiences—good and bad—that shaped my leadership skills.

It is commonly held that you should be discerning in choosing your role models and surrounding yourself with those who help you grow into a better person. Though oversimplifying, I've heard it said, "You are the average of your four best friends." Surrounding ourselves with people who make us better—and identifying role models similarly—is critical for all of us to be our best selves and to be the best leaders we can be.

Perhaps what is not discussed as much when addressing the subject of role models is that you can and should learn from all the people that you encounter. In developing leadership skills, you will learn from effective leaders and I would argue you can learn every bit as much from ineffective ones.

My wife Patti and I have six children, two of whom, like me, started their professional careers as CPAs in a public accounting firm. Public accounting is a great place to develop technical skills, but with the right attitude, perhaps a better place to develop leadership and people skills. Unlike with most jobs, a developing CPA will frequently rotate clients—and the partners, managers, and senior leaders that serve each client. This means that you have the opportunity to work with many different "bosses" and in different client situations. I remember several discussions with Luke and Katie when they were complaining about their current "boss." I would always coach them to cherish unpleasant leaders as much as pleasant ones and to chalk those negative experiences up to this category: *"things I won't emulate in developing my leadership style."*

So, the qualities of leadership are truly not much different than the qualities of life… developing our personality and values… our Brand… as each of us chooses the manner in which we live and treat others.

So let me tell you a little bit more about my own experiences and learnings in my life. I always hesitate to elaborate on these things of the soul, as I don't want to appear to be bragging about my accomplishments or think for one second that "I've figured this out" (because I know that I will die without "figuring this out"). What I am really describing are the many blessings that God has given me in my life. And I appreciate the opportunity to share these blessings with others.

My father, Clement, died on October 25, 2006, seven days before his 91st birthday—at least according to his birth certificate and my Grandma Catherine. You see, Dad was actually born late on the day of October 31, 1915, and my devout grandmother was able to talk the doctor into establishing November 1st, All Saints' Day, as his date of birth.

At the time of this writing, my mother is 103, still living on her own and thriving. Of her 91 living descendants and their families, Mom can tell you today what each one is doing with their lives at this moment. An amazing woman who has lived a life of faith and service and was a great role model for me. Mom was a super-organized CEO of her household of twelve and a model for any woman striving to be a great wife and mother.

Dad had a fourth-grade education, and my mother had an eighth-grade education. Did either ever write an autobiography or pontificate about leadership? Well, actually, my mother did! At the age of 100, my brother David collaborated with Mom on her life story, entitled *100 Years from Now... A Memoir*, which is mostly about her life experiences and not much in the way of providing earthly advice—she is much too humble for that! By the way, it's a great read! I highly recommend it! Though neither of my parents would have thought for a second that they were "leadership gurus," they were the most impactful mentors and leaders in my life.

My grandparents were immigrants to the U.S. My Grandma Catherine actually gave birth to my uncle Jake, their first child, on a boat during her journey to America.

My parents and grandparents knew nothing but hard work and discipline and were great stewards of the limited resources they were given. They were family- and faith-centered and bestowed this great blessing on me and my siblings.

My parents were part of what I believe was the best generation in the U.S.—the Depression era. They experienced difficult times in an era well before the Industrial Revolution and were completely foreign to all of the conveniences we have today. They were great stewards of limited resources, with an emphasis on faith, family, and communities. They were hard-working, disciplined, and focused on the aforementioned—which we would all agree are the things that matter the most.

Clearly, they were—and are—amazing people, but as I said at the onset, we are all shaped by our own experiences and mentors in our lives.

I have also been blessed to travel internationally in my business and have met people from all over the world who are like this "best generation in the U.S.," And I've come to realize that you will often find these people in countries that are poorer and underdeveloped—possessing a greater focus on what's most important: faith, family, and community.

In our developed world (e.g., in Western societies), we have so much that we tend to get distracted. We get further and further away from those things that are most important… and from our faith. In short, we're too fat and happy. We get caught up in today's social norms around what is important. I've learned that we need to be deliberate about focusing on our faith, our loved ones, and others. I've also learned not to get enamored with ourselves and the many things that attempt to define "success" in our developed world. I believe that this mindset will lead to a more fulfilled existence and a happier one! And it will make you a better leader.

To give you more insight into some of my role models, I'd like to share some notable quotes from growing up.

"We couldn't move in with our folks because they were still living with their folks."

My dad had a lot of one-liners that our family has memorialized as "Clemisms." This quote is one of them, as he would always joke about how poor he and Mom were when they were married. It wasn't exactly true, but when my parents got married, they couldn't afford to live independently, so they initially lived with my dad's parents.

Growing up, Dad was taunted and bullied in school. He was cross-eyed because his parents couldn't afford corrective lenses, and he was labeled a "beet weeder" because they were migrant workers. The entire family was engaged in working the beet fields. He had to finish school after the fourth grade. Think of that! At nine or ten years old, he was expected to work full-time with his family in the beet fields.

With a mere fourth-grade education, Dad didn't have a lot of job opportunities.

"If I had a high school diploma, I'd be the janitor at the Britt church."

So, Dad really had a hard time getting a job. He went to apply for a job at a local church in his hometown of Britt, Iowa, to be a janitor. And they wouldn't hire him because he didn't have a high school diploma. Later, Dad joked that if he had gotten a high school diploma, he'd be the janitor at this church.

Dad got a break in a Maytag dealership, initially repairing and delivering the first automatic washing machines of his time, and worked very hard. His customer skills were noted because he was *simply a servant* who cared only about taking care of his customers—honestly and wholeheartedly—and he eventually transitioned into a sales role. His success in sales landed him a sales position in home improvement products—home insulation and siding. Eventually, he started his own business with two partners and made a good living to support his outsized family.

"Don't light the candle on both ends and burn it in the middle."

Dad would describe much of his work career in this manner. In the age before electricity (something my parents experienced), people would use the phrase "light the candle on both ends" to describe working morning and night. Dad took this phrase a step further, adding "burn the candle in the middle" in his description of his career. Later, Dad warned me that working hard is a great virtue, but having a balance with faith and family is important.

"What you give to the Lord, you get back double."

If there was someone I met in my life who may have worked harder than my dad, it was my Grandma Catherine. With Grandpa William, she immigrated from Russia, where Catherine the Great had recruited industrious farming families from Germany to farm the Volga River basin. Once in Russia, they were oppressed and fled to the U.S. I just can't imagine how brave they were to come to this country. They had nothing. They knew no one. They couldn't speak the language. And Grandma was weeks from giving birth to their first child. "Wow" is an understatement.

My grandpa never really spoke any English, so my interaction with him was seeing that huge smile that covered his face and his open arms as I ran into their home from our car during a Sunday visit and jumped onto his lap. It was enough. Words didn't really matter. Grandma, on the other hand, learned the language and adapted to her new country to make a home for her family.

Among other things, Grandma had a huge vegetable garden that she worked to feed her family and, as it turned out, much of the town of Britt. She gave away much even though she had so little. And I'll never forget visiting her on Sunday and hearing my aunt scolding her for giving vegetables and money away. She would say, "Ma, you can't afford that!" And Grandma would reply in her beautiful broken English, *"What you give to the Lord, you get back double."*

Throughout my life, I have watched those words happen time and time again. My grandparents and parents demonstrated it often, and I've seen it happen in my own life.

"Say, do you need any folding money?"

One of my dad's ways of offering help to someone in need was uttering this phrase… because they didn't have Venmo in those days! I heard him say this often, and he offered a lot of help to family and friends in need during his life—including his own ten children.

Mom and Dad were very successful in the ways that really matter. Their primary objective was to raise their children and provide them with a Christian education that neither one of them could afford, and realized they were disadvantaged as they lived their lives. (Not only did they put their ten children through Catholic school, but eight of us through college. One sister who did not choose college chose beauty school and went on to be the owner of her own shop. An older brother suffered from mental illness and taught me more about character and perseverance than I could ever aptly capture in this chapter—or in several books.) Post-retirement, Mom and Dad donated their farm to Newman Catholic Schools to kick off a campaign to build a new elementary school. I have just described two lifetimes of generosity and service.

"Don't throw your weight around."

As my parents got older and were recognized a bit for this success, we heard this frequently from Dad. It was his fourth-grade-educated way of saying, "Be humble." I believe humility is one of the greatest virtues.

Culture and Values

You probably have guessed by now that your *Brand* and establishing the right *Culture* is most important in leading a team.

What do I mean by Brand and Culture? This isn't a logo, aspirational mission statement, and/or core values that so many organizations lean behind and use to provide lip service. Instead, it is truly who you are. For an organization, it describes its true mojo—what everyone aligns to strive to be and how we show up for work every day. You caught elements of the Brands of my parents and grandparents in what I have shared with you about their lives and their values—in how they lived and what they did that mattered.

For NutriQuest, my primary business, our Brand Promise is *"Ingenuity Inspired by Servitude,"* and our North Star is to be *"The Most Trusted."* That coveted trust is further defined by both integrity and competency.

Core Values of NutriQuest

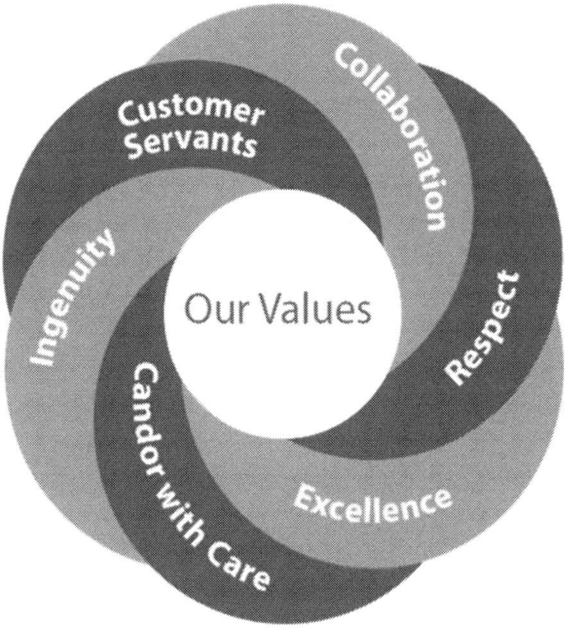

So, how do you effectively establish a strong brand and culture?

Again, for me, it is the most critical element of leading a team.

First, as a leader, you need to *walk the walk*. You need to live and breathe these values in your actions. Every single person in your organization is watching you. They are following your cue. You are, by virtue of your role, their role model and mentor. Think about that for a minute. Let it sink in. That is an awesome and daunting responsibility—and one you signed up for as their leader. First and foremost, your organization's Brand and Culture starts with you.

Secondly, you need to be intentional, particularly as your organization grows in size. Creating and living a culture was easy at NutriQuest when there were just eight to ten of us. It consisted of our other leaders and me interacting frequently with everyone on the team. However, as we grew, we needed to be intentional about discussing and celebrating our chosen values, as well as making sure our key decisions were aligned with those values.

We attempt to achieve this in several ways. We emphasize discussing and sharing these core values in all internal presentations and meetings. So, the above depiction of our Core Values, our Brand Promise, and North Star are always seen and acknowledged throughout the organization. Our quarterly check-ins and annual performance evaluations incorporate each core value as a measurement of performance. How do our team members demonstrate each of our core values?

We have developed a recognition system for everyone in our organization. All team members are given the opportunity to nominate their colleagues for *Servitude*, *Ingenuity*, and *Collaboration* awards. With this nomination, we ask them to outline their best case as to why that team member should be recognized. In addition, we have developed an annual award program to recognize these quarterly award winners and celebrate the team members who best exemplified our core values that year. These are coveted awards at NutriQuest.

Servant Leadership

I have already mentioned the James Hunter book, which was inspiring to me, and a book that NutriQuest leaders read and discuss. Some elements of servant leadership that I think are most critical within these principles are as follows, with brief explanations.

To Whom Much is Given, Much is Expected: As someone who has aspired to be a leader, you have been very blessed. And it is important to literally count (and recount) your many blessings and thank God for them. I, for one, do not do this enough. I have learned that the best way to give thanks is to recognize that, because of those many blessings, much is expected from us as leaders. It is imperative that we find ways to give back. The expectation of a leader is to live and breathe high standards as a role model for his or her organization. That also entails being generous to others.

Work Hard, With Discipline, With Passion: Like my father and grandmother before me, I have aspired to work hard. But what about the importance of work-life balance? Honestly, to be an effective leader, this is important—especially important to promote among your people. But a *healthy imbalance* is truly the right balance. Let me elaborate.

You and I have both known leaders who, when promoted to a management position, believe that they no longer need to do the work. They can sit back and direct. Clearly, stepping back more and "directing" is important in that step to a leadership position. But getting your hands dirty, helping solve complex problems, and being arm-in-arm with your people is critical in providing effective leadership.

When you think about the most accomplished people in this world—those who you might choose to emulate as a person and a leader—how many of them had a "50/50" work-life balance? Christ? Mother Teresa? Michael Jordan? How about successful leaders in the U.S. swine industry? To name just a few: Jeff Hansen, Bob Christensen, John Schwartz, Pat Hord? All are great examples of an imbalance inherent in the drive to be the best.

I also can't underemphasize the *Discipline* and *Passion* that are essential to this ethic. The old adage "Work smarter, not harder" is so true. The principles of discipline and organization—planning, setting goals, measuring progress, executing, holding yourself and your organization accountable, and (yes) sweating the details—are critical. To the latter point, when I hear some leaders say that they are "strategic leaders" and "not good at details," right or wrong, that probably translates into the words "I am lazy." Having the discipline to "sweat the details" along with your team to achieve excellence is important.

And *Passion* is how you show up—always being positive, energetic, committed. And displaying that passion, particularly toward your people and your customers, who are your highest priority. I absolutely love the key core value of our Hoover's Hatchery business. It is *Tenacity*. I am so proud of the team at our hatcheries. They move heaven and earth every day to deliver exceptional customer service. There is no such thing as "we can't do this," but instead, "here's how we will do this" in solving problems and innovating. Tenacity combines discipline and passion to never take no for an answer and not settle for being second best.

My father, the cross-eyed (but handsome) "beet weeder" with a fourth-grade education, forged a successful career in service. He raised ten children whom he sent through Catholic school and college. *He* exemplified tenacity.

Serve Others; All are Above You: Many leaders have the traditional pyramid of leadership hierarchy completely backward. The traditional organizational chart (with many workers at the bottom of a pyramid narrowing through each level of management until reaching the peak of the pyramid with the CEO on top) needs to be flipped upside down in terms of how we think, work, and treat each other.

As a leader, I believe that you should place yourself second to your customers and your people. The ultimate act of leadership was demonstrated by Christ when he washed the feet of his faithful twelve. It was the most lowly, menial task of that age. Lead like all are above you. Serve your people by your example. Demonstrate generosity by providing adequate tools and feedback. Help them develop by caring about their families and their work-life balance.

And yes, provide accountability. Help them strive to contribute to the best of their abilities, and correct and guide them when they are faltering. Our *Candor with Care* core value is meant to emphasize the importance of this element and give our people at all levels the authority—rather, the responsibility—to hold each other to high standards. Use candor to be honest, and forthright in correcting poor behaviour out of love for that person, and show mutual love and respect for the people that make up your organization. The "with care" element means to do so in a manner that is not condescending or harsh but rather enabling and constructive.

Meet People Where They Are: As important as *Candor* is in addressing behaviours honestly with those you lead, it is also critical to be empathetic and meet individuals where they are. There is an Indian proverb that goes like this: *"Never judge the soul of a man until you've walked two moons in his moccasins."* Always lead with trust that people are well-intentioned and have a myriad of elements influencing their behaviour. Of course, when trust is breached, you need to call it out and hold them accountable. Though you'll never fully understand each person and their behaviour, seek to understand and articulate that you want to believe in them. You trust them. You want nothing more than to help them be successful.

Think Long Term vs. Transactional: The most successful organizations think long term in their decision-making orientation, development of strategies, and ultimately in execution. And though executing every transaction of every day with discipline is important, a transactional "win-lose" approach in the day-to-day will never allow you to achieve long-term success.

What do I mean by not thinking transactional? For me, win-win is table stakes. But for our businesses, achieving long-term success means giving more than that. It means going beyond win-win—to create that North Star of trust that inspires loyalty and satisfying, mutually beneficial, long-lasting relationships. For your people, it results in retention and high levels of engagement. For your customers, trust means that they may favor your products and services above others and give you the benefit of the doubt. For your suppliers, it inspires a similar giving attitude to collaborate in solving your problems and those of your customers. But only if trust is real and earned—every day. This happens only when the leader:

- Gives more than he/she receives.
- Sacrifices short-term for long-term gain.
- Goes beyond win-win to create long-term value.

Financial and Operating Discipline: What about execution? When I emphasize *"Think Long Term,"* I am not suggesting that organizations must have a formal long-term strategic plan that they follow with devotion, which is perhaps contrary to popular opinion among business leaders. Secondly, I am not saying abandon short-term thinking. What I am suggesting is to have a mindset of achieving long-term success and sustainability in everything you do.

Making it Up as You Go: One of the quotes that I have used frequently with my leadership team when we talk about our direction and long-term planning (and it sometimes drives them crazy) is *"Not sure what we should do. We're making this up as we go!"* Long-term planning to me is overrated. You must have a long-term vision for what you want to achieve, but it is often said that a long-term plan is obsolete the day that it is printed. That is because, today, more than ever, the realities of our business change frequently and materially, rendering formal long-term "road maps" obsolete. Successful organizations adopt a long-term vision but are nimble and entrepreneurial to pivot to these fundamental changes in order to achieve success.

Financial Planning/Goal Setting: Successful organizations condense their long-term plan (to the extent that it exists) to an annual plan and ultimately to short-term (ideally daily and weekly) KPIs (Key Performance Indicators) and goals. Achievement of these goals is then measured and reported to drive accountability to the organization. This is a key element of financial and operating discipline.

For me, it's important to take a bottom-up approach when putting together an operating plan. Assigning P&L (Profit and Loss) responsibility to managers who oversee farms or other independent operations is important for the best relevancy and fundamentals of developing those leaders. The plan should be driven by key operating drivers—the KPIs—more so than financial ones and should be created by the individual operating managers, reviewed by their supervisors, and ultimately approved by finance and senior leadership. The end result consists of weekly goals by farm/operating units for both KPIs and revenue and expense line items. Note also that some KPIs (e.g., customer service scores, engagement scores, other people-related scores such as turnover or safety) do not tie directly to financial performance but cannot be underemphasized in this process.

Reporting and Benchmarking: With the bottoms-up financial plan complete, you have the tools for daily, weekly, and monthly reporting of key KPIs and line-item financial parameters.

To have value, information must be timely, accurate, and relevant. Accuracy should be table stakes and needs to be driven by the organization, stressing the importance of operating and financial parameters. Weekly reporting that is promptly produced while things are fresh and consist of the most important and relevant operating and financial metrics is a key element. Many organizations are becoming more astute at weekly scorecards.

Delivering these key metrics to the right audience—those who can impact the outcome—is also a key parameter. I've witnessed some organizations that get the reporting right but communicate only to higher levels in the organization, even KPI information, but especially financial information. The thinking that financial results should, for some reason, be privy only to "management" is a mistake.

In terms of relevancy, while business intelligence and AI (Artificial Intelligence) tools have outstanding potential to provide relevance, these too are often geared toward "management." I would also argue that low-tech can be every bit as effective. The most effective communication of results that I've witnessed in an organization was in a U.S. sow farm. Visiting one of our farms at Iowa Select Farms, where I served as CFO, I witnessed the manager sitting around the room during a shared break with farm workers. During that break, he walked methodically to a whiteboard. With a black marker, he wrote each KPI representing that day's results next to the goal and prior days' results for those same KPIs. Note that 100% of the data collection, recording, and reporting was done by hand. Two workers made very relevant points, and that day's activity versus the target was discussed, including what was to happen tomorrow. Timeliness is a key element of relevance—and relevance, of course, relates to reporting and communication in such a way that it is actionable and can impact results.

Evaluate and Understand: Just as the farm workers engaged in their daily discussion, which provided the impetus to meet or exceed that day's and week's goals, there needs to be an understood process of evaluating and understanding the results. Clearly and intentionally, getting the right information to the right individuals who can affect change will result in improved performance. This is where my earlier point of budgeting from the bottom up comes in—identifying goals at every level of the organization. At the senior level, C-suite directors are looking at company-level performance. Operating leaders are equipped with performance measurements versus goals at each level. Together, all are evaluating performance, understanding the key drivers, and ultimately implementing the appropriate measures for improvement.

Here again, it is important to focus on the highest-impact KPIs and also on controllable factors. Don't waste time chasing pennies, and consider not even sharing the non-controllable variables with lower-level managers. Focus on what can most impact the organization and what can best be controlled.

Success Is Profitability and Sustainability: Ultimately, all of these disciplines are geared to maximize profitability and, therefore, long-term success and sustainability of the business. Profitability is vital to any business's ability to continue to contribute to society and should be the just reward— even a scorecard of sorts—for the leaders and owners of the business.

People Leadership

Successful leadership to me is entirely measured by the effectiveness of people leadership. That is why I started this chapter emphasizing *Culture* and *Servant Leadership*, two of the most important principles of people leadership. I will address some other important elements of people leadership.

Deliberate Hiring: Talent and Fit: Building a team starts with recruitment—attracting the right people to join your organization. Every business I've ever worked for has its own approach to accomplishing this. But the most successful ones have a positive Culture and Brand that is a magnet for those who are a fit. This comes back to all of the things that I spoke about at the beginning of this chapter. For those who don't want to be part of your Brand and Culture, guess what? You don't want them. They just won't fit. Obviously, it is also important to hire the right talent and competencies. However, it is easier to develop competency than it is to mold a square peg into a round hole culturally. Start with the people in your organization who do fit, and promote referrals. Offer a bonus for referrals that lead to a new hire and some length of service.

High Expectations, High Reward: I have always tried to set the standard of high expectations in terms of drive, commitment, and passion. As a leader, you must *walk the walk*. Everyone wants to be part of a winning organization—one that is not only profitable but can demonstrate that its customers and industry benefit greatly from its goods and services. Don't be afraid to set high expectations for performance—*"Winning teams must do this!"*—but couple it with recognition and high rewards.

View payroll expense as an investment versus an expense, and develop bonus systems that reward the right behaviour aligned with the organization's long-term goals. That doesn't mean avoiding short-term goals, as they are stepping stones to long-term sustainability. But if you believe, like me, that the most successful organizations think long-term in their execution and decision-making, design reward systems with that in mind. It is well understood that reward systems—bonuses—will drive performance. So, be careful what you wish for and what behaviours you are rewarding. You must be very thoughtful and deliberate in designing these packages and celebrate when you grant out-sized bonuses to individuals who earn them.

Entrepreneurial Culture: Regardless of the size of your organization, foster a continuous improvement culture that rewards ingenuity and encourages risk-taking. That also means you have to accept failure. Create a culture and processes that ideally achieve "fail fast." At NutriQuest, we have the privilege of doing discovery and innovation work, which involves constantly developing business cases and testing many different technologies—most of which fail. It's easy to celebrate those technologies that get launched and are successful in the marketplace, but we always endeavor to praise the team when we "deep-six" a project, particularly when it is early in the process. It means our process worked. Our iterative development process is designed to identify, as early as we can, whether a technology will ultimately be a winner or not.

Path to Ownership: You know by now that I am a huge believer in long-term alignment within the organization. You achieve this with Culture, you achieve it with your rewards system, and you can especially achieve it by providing a path to ownership for your key people. Here again, we have developed, with deliberateness, a set of performance and impact (not tenure) criteria that provide an opportunity for equity ownership in the business.

I have also helped companies do this with a "phantom equity" bonus plan, taking into account profitability and increases in the value of the business. But to me, there is nothing like real ownership—the kind that requires an investment and "skin in the game" as units of equity are issued. For key people who are younger in their careers, making it difficult to write a sizable check for equity, we will sometimes provide loans. We have also developed a *Profits Interest* ownership mechanism that works like a stock option, providing equity upside on any increases in the value of the equity of the business. Here again, the devil's in the details with the "golden handcuff" components of ownership, which are captured in an organization's Operating Agreement and Buy-Sell Agreement. When done well, the equity ownership mechanism—more than any other—achieves the alignment and motivation for your key people.

In addition to long-term alignment, the ownership element is a development opportunity in understanding financial statements, income tax implications, and how to make strategic decisions for the business.

Intentional Tools: There are some great tools for people management, many of which I learned from the 21st-century Ag Leadership program. I have been able to help in a small way in developing a curriculum for the program and have had an up-and-coming leader from our NutriQuest or Hoover's business attend nearly all of the cohort leadership groups that have been conducted to date. Stating the obvious and putting my money where my mouth is, I am a huge believer in this program.

Some of these tools include *DISC*, for which the "Platinum Rule" is a simple but brilliant concept. Going beyond the centuries-old "Golden Rule" to treat others the way *you* want to be treated emphasizes the importance of achieving a level of understanding of each person so that you can try to treat others the way *they* want to be treated.

Kinlaw's Four Pillars and *Franklin Covey's Four Disciplines of Execution* ("4DX") also come to mind as great tools for engagement and disciplined execution. Creating a culture of commitment to Kinlaw's four pillars—*clarity, competence, influence,* and *appreciation*—creates the cultural foundation to drive performance. Covey's four disciplines go beyond cultural elements to execution by defining the most important goals, focusing on leading (versus lagging) measures and driving a cadence of accountability with targeted scorecards and weekly meetings.

Employee Engagement Surveys are also an important tool. The old adage *"If you don't measure it, you won't improve it"* really holds true—not just in KPI and financial measures, but in people measures. Assigning a numeric score to employee engagement is a barometer (not a hard-and-fast objective number), which is very effective when measured consistently over time (e.g., every quarter or every six months). Reviewing this on a departmental basis and reviewing the comments shared carefully are very effective tools in understanding what is probably the most important measurement for a business: employee morale and engagement. We review these carefully and couple each review with substantive action plans to improve engagement. And believe me, there is always plenty of room for improvement.

Provide Leadership Training: Honestly, Ben Woolley did not make me write this or know that I would write this when he asked me to write a chapter for this book. Here again, being deliberate and intentional about developing leaders is critical. I'm sure there are many great leadership programs out there, but the 21st-century Ag Leadership course has been invaluable to our organizations. Leadership really *is* learned. You're not born with it, and you don't develop it fully on your own. Not only is the coursework valuable, but my colleagues who have benefited from this program have greatly benefited from their peers in the course. Leadership can be lonely, and there are many times when you don't want to discuss certain elements with others in your organization. So, having peers in other companies with whom you can share your leadership journey is invaluable. I, too, have deliberated on identifying friends who lead other businesses. Many are in different industries. We deliberately engage in meetings regularly to learn from each other.

Table Stakes: All of these tools and approaches are elements of some of the most obvious—but often most fumbled—elements of leadership. These include:

- **Strive to be the Best at Everything You Do**: In addition to the obvious, it's important to focus your organization's efforts on what it truly can be best at—shying away from initiatives where that is not the case unless they add to the bigger picture.
- **Work with Discipline, Be Deliberate, Have Tenacity**: Leadership isn't just about leading and inspiring people to be engaged. It's about execution. Being a leader doesn't just happen. Good leaders make it happen by being very intentional—modeling *Discipline* and *Tenacity*. That means sweating the details.
- **Look in the Mirror**: As a leader and in establishing the culture of your organization, always look in the mirror before blaming external factors in assessing failure or opportunities to improve. This is core to accountability and fundamental to affecting change.
- **Anxious Is Good**: I am, by nature, a nervous person who has what I hope is a healthy paranoia that things can always

be better. I get very concerned when I hear of parents wanting their children to take anxiety medication because they are anxious. Don't get me wrong—I know mental illness, and I appreciate its real impact and the need for treatment. But I think in many (most?) cases, anxiety is a good thing. It pushes us to improve and never settle and to avoid complacency—which, to me, is a dirty word.

- **Heart and Head**: Successful leaders are able to combine the *Culture* and *Servant Leadership* elements with the discipline-in-execution elements. Both are important. And everyone wants to be part of a winning team that is making a positive difference.

Conclusion

I hope that some of the people I've been honored to lead in the past have had a chance to read this. And I guarantee you that if you are one of these people, you are apt to be thinking, *"I don't remember Steve leading in this way."* Even more likely, you can recount the many mistakes that I made along this journey.

That is because the path to effective leadership is a journey. It is exactly the same as the path to being a better person, a better Christian. We all stumble along the way. It is so important to never think for a second that *"you've arrived"*—but instead, that you need to pay close attention to how you can grow as a better person, a better leader.

I learned that someone had suggested the process of doing a crossword puzzle as a model for understanding life's (and I'd add leadership's) growth journey, in that it's *"arrogant to do it in pen."* First, you should draw it with a pencil. You will most likely find out something new that will require changing the original guess. Figuring out life—and leadership—is like that also.

At the age of 62, I feel that I have gained a certain amount of wisdom and experience from life's experiences, the many blessings that I've shared with you in this chapter. I especially know that I need to strive to continue to learn and grow more as a person in order to become a better person, a better Christian, a better *Servant*. To me, that is the key to effective leadership.

Chapter 3: Lessons in Leadership

Collette Kaster

Collette Kaster has a passion for improving animal agriculture and showing people all the great opportunities it can offer. She loves to help people better understand how food is produced and the role of meat in the diet.

After 25 years of experience in the meat industry, leading large teams in the areas of technical services and livestock procurement, she currently serves as the CEO of the American Meat Science Association (AMSA) as well as the Executive Director for the Professional Animal Auditor Certification Organization (PAACO). She is an AMSA Fellow and has served on the Advisory Committee for Meat and Poultry Inspection. She currently serves on many association and company advisory committees in the areas of animal welfare, food safety, and meat quality.

Outside of work, she and her husband, Dennis, reside outside of Kansas City and stay busy with family, dogs, and a cow herd.

A little about me. My path is not a straight one. As I grew up, I wanted to be an archaeologist, then a horse trainer, and then a graphic designer (before that was a thing, personal computers were widely used). Beginning at age 14, I worked as a waitress, bartender, and prep cook, riding a small motorcycle down a couple miles of an Iowa gravel road to get to work. I graduated high school a month after turning 16 and entered college that fall as an art major. I quickly realized that art was not my calling and became an early adopter of the gap year concept, which I took between my freshman and sophomore years. I spent that time traveling with my grandparents and exploring other colleges and majors along the way, landing in California to stay with my dad and learning a lot of life lessons working at a startup restaurant.

My love for livestock started with horses. We raised and showed them successfully on a shoestring budget, including riding horses for others to get an opportunity to gain experience. I have no doubt that if equine management had been a major at any of the schools I explored (which it is at all of them now), I would have chosen that path and ended up financially broke or physically broken—or both! Instead, I leaned into the love of livestock I had developed by helping at my grandparents' diversified farm and chose animal science. This choice took me down a path I could not have imagined. Like many of my meat science colleagues, I was introduced to it through a great teacher (Bill Costello at SDSU) and through meat judging. As we traveled endless miles in the meat judging van, I found the meat industry endlessly fascinating—with its history and complexity—and it's been a great place to build a career and meet some of the best friends and colleagues.

As someone who was labeled "bossy" at a very early age, it's always hard for me to sort out nature vs. nurture as it pertains to leadership. There's no doubt that taking ownership and making decisions comes much easier to some than others, and it took me a while to figure out that these were skills I could put to good use. I have been fortunate in these attributes, as well as the fact that I'm an extrovert and suffer greatly from FOMO (fear of missing out).

I also have a high degree of curiosity about almost everything and love to dig in and understand a variety of useful and not-so-useful topics. In any personality assessment, I tend to score high in the "D" category or "red," which typically means I am direct, results-driven, and assertive. Because of these traits, I sometimes find it challenging to work with others who have a different approach or pace. But as a good colleague once said, we need the thinkers and the doers—and some of us are fortunate to be both.

My faults are many… I am impatient, I have too frequently had a need to be right, and I have erred toward being defensive. These have been a problem for me at times with family members and team members. I typically have been able to tamp this down as it relates to those charged with leading me, but even then, it can manifest as undermining their direction. In my early career, I thought my educational expertise (M.S. in meat science) trumped some of my coworkers' years of applied/learned experience in that same area. I was fortunate that I had kind, patient, generous leaders to mentor me to a place of improved teamwork and humility.

As my career and life have progressed, I've relied more on outside perspectives, friends, and mentors, and I feel confident seeking input from a broad caucus—even if I don't agree with them on everything. My current role in association leadership works well because these organizations are run by boards of directors whose members have many different outlooks. It is very rewarding to work collaboratively with these groups on behalf of the entire organization.

Finding synergies and capitalizing on them, along with reducing or eliminating redundancies, are important to me and have served me well. In fact, I've been a little obsessed with efficiency since I was young, when I would try to do any basic chore in the most systematic way possible with no backtracking—sometimes timing myself. When I recently shared this with my sister, she responded, "Well, that explains a lot..." Finding efficiencies and synergy while reducing redundancy can drive a lot of productivity.

I had a mentor tell me early on to "know my numbers," which is critical for understanding and measuring what you do and how to develop its value and priority. Identifying key metrics is crucial for effective communication with a team and driving progress. While leaders must have a clear vision for their team, organization, and mission, they also need a solid grasp of the work they expect others to accomplish. This approach can be liberating and usually something people find valuable. Team members know they are expected to execute—or have a valid reason why something shouldn't be done—and an alternative plan to accomplish or reshape the objective. Creating a shared vision is so valuable, and even more so now that I lead board-directed organizations overseen by board members with diverse experiences and roles.

Establishing numerical and measurable goals is sometimes not easy, particularly if you are working in a support function; I speak from experience on this one! In that case, you may be a contributor to a numerical goal, or yours may be more qualitative in nature with time-based measurements. It's always critical to ask yourself or your team, *Why are you doing this?* Activity does not always equal accomplishment. A hard pill to swallow for the tactical person who relishes a good to-do list.

I enjoy and value finding the best in people and helping them be successful, even when they don't think they can do some of the things I've put in front of them. Coalescing people into a team with shared goals is very rewarding, and it's possible for all of us to do much more than we think we can do. To accomplish this, teams need trust, which comes from creating an environment where people can speak freely and state any considerations and where they have respect for one another. I will add an important caveat to this—and that is, I have very little tolerance for complaining. It is important to bring solutions, or at least ideas, when you are discussing challenges and problems. It's definitely an expectation that each person carries their weight and has a solid understanding of their areas.

A little about women in ag and positions of leadership. This has changed so much during my career, and I'm very thankful for that. It's no secret that the meat industry and agriculture have been male-dominated and continue to be so at the highest level. However, things are changing, and there is a greater understanding of individual needs and creating careers and solutions that work. It's become more acceptable for everyone to prioritize family and associated activities, whether you are male or female. When my oldest daughter reached high school and was a talented softball player, I remember my boss asking me incredulously if I planned on leaving early (4 p.m.) for all games?! As someone who traveled at least 50% of my work time, I responded that yes, in fact, I did plan to attend every game that I could. He later went through a critical issue with one of his children and subsequently apologized to me for not having the right perspective.

I have a work-hard, play-hard mindset and look for others who operate the same way. In some roles, if the work gets done, there's room for schedule flexibility. However, in manufacturing and operations, fixed shifts are necessary, leaving less room for that flexibility. Many businesses are trying to build elements of flexibility into these roles to accommodate a shrinking workforce. I often included my children in my business travel and even the business itself, introducing them to coworkers and unique situations. I hope this helped prepare them to interact confidently with adults, to see what their mom was doing, and to teach them a little about how to act in certain situations. I fully recognize I crafted my career to facilitate that, and I definitely made sacrifices—including turning down some roles that were operational in nature, as I felt that would reduce my availability and flexibility for them. As I said in one resignation letter, *"There are many things you can do again or do differently... parenting is not typically one of them."*

One of the most impactful things I ever did for my career was apply for a job outside my discipline (marketing), which was a lateral move. I did not get the job, but shortly thereafter, my boss called me into his office and offered me a much bigger stretch job with high visibility and accountability. Had I not indicated my openness to new things, I'm not sure I would have entered his thought process for a new role. Lesson learned: we *can* do hard things—even things we are not sure we are ready for—especially if we can lean on a team and be humble about what we do and don't know.

I take great pleasure in seeing that more roles in operations and sales are now crafted in a way that recognizes the need for both men and women to have flexibility and value time spent with family. The term *work-life balance* can be useful if you realize that it's not always 50/50 or a fixed situation. You might spend some days or weeks immersed in a project or solving a complex problem and have to reconnect later with some downtime or vacation days with your family.

If you are leaving, leave when things are good, not when they're bad. When I had what I joked about as my "mid-life" crisis, I left a very large company where I held a senior leadership position, managed large teams I literally loved, and had a great relationship with coworkers. I left to begin association work—something I had considered occasionally—and that presented itself to me right as my kids were entering high school. I left a high-profile, highly compensated role with all the perks for a role that paid a fraction of the salary and required me to create all infrastructure (accounting, payroll, HR, IT, phone, office, etc.). It was certainly a bit of a culture shock, but it allowed for tremendous autonomy and the chance to reimagine not one but two organizations.

However, women are still frequently choosing to stop the progression of their careers before reaching the highest levels of senior leadership for most operational roles. There are many senior leaders in HR, IT, legal, and technical fields but fewer in finance, ops, and sales. Whether we want to admit it or not, there are still examples of discrimination in treatment—and especially pay and job titles. Those who serve as mentors for women need to facilitate this transition and help bring women to the table.

Own your destiny. Don't be a victim or a martyr. This is a habit one can fall into. The culture of "busyness" requires us to all relate how uniquely busy and overwhelmed we are—as a race to the bottom. I recently did some executive coaching and was quite shocked to be called out as having some victim mentalities. I saw that my need to control and do everything was leading me to be a martyr, which was thinly disguised as being a victim. I have been working hard to get out of that place and am much less defensive. This has really worked well, especially at home, where my interactions had fallen into this bad habit.

I have also been spending time recently in the Stoic philosophy, and I find it so beneficial not to get pulled into all of the outrage that is so prevalent now. We can only truly control ourselves and our reactions—and all of the complaining and doomsaying serves no benefit.

It's fascinating to be in the latter stages of my career and to begin to think about what retirement from conventional work would be like for me. Most people think it would be very difficult for me not to work, but I have no doubt I could find many other places to channel energy and effort through volunteer organizations.

Main Messages

1. **Work hard.** Sounds so obvious, but being known for hard work and dedication to completing a task is a superpower that will open many doors. It's rewarding—and my number one piece of advice to my children and what I try to model not just at work but in life.

2. **Be a lifelong learner.** This takes curiosity and time. We have more information at hand than ever. Ask the hard questions. One of my favorite things that someone shared recently about me was that he appreciated I was always willing to ask the question that everyone wanted to know but was afraid to ask.

3. **Leaders should be knowledgeable of the areas they oversee** but stay out of the details and let good people

manage their areas, make recommendations, and provide solutions.

4. **Champion the underdog—or someone who needs and deserves support and a chance.** Find ways to grow people and give them opportunities. Reward them for that with pay and praise. Andy Reid said, *"Don't put people in a box—they might surprise you,"* and that has been my experience. Withhold judgment or the obvious impression.

5. **Be genuine and unique,** but it's also necessary to fit into your environment to be effective. If you can't do that, find a different environment.

6. **Be concise.** Women often add too many details, and men often speak in soundbites. Your message may get lost, and you might later hear someone say the exact same thing you just did—but in a more effective manner that gets heard.

7. **Don't fill the silence.** Practice the pause. Very difficult to do (for me), but highly useful.

8. **Gratitude.** Have it and express it.

9. **Attributes I find useful:** curiosity, empathy (although I am subject to compassion fatigue), candidness, directness, and backing up what you know with facts—not supposition.

10. **Grow your network.** Knowing who to call is invaluable.
11. **Be absolutely trustworthy** and someone who can be counted upon. Times when I have failed at this have been my most regretful moments.
12. **There are no do-overs.** Listen to your heart and instinct. Make changes if you want or need to.

Chapter 4: Leading Through Legacy and Innovation

Randy Stoecker

Randy Stoecker is one of the most respected and forward-thinking leaders in the pig industry.

Randy grew up in Kansas and was instrumental in the early growth of PIC in the United States.

He then went on to become President of Murphy Farm West and pioneered the use of contract finishing across the Midwest. Family farmers owe a huge debt of gratitude to Randy for providing them with an alternative stream of income.

Leadership's Role in Successful Businesses

I was fortunate to enjoy a 45-year career in Agribusiness, primarily involved with the swine industry, both in the breeding stock as well as the commercial production and processing sectors. During that period, the US and much of the developed world's swine industry underwent significant changes in financially important genetic improvements, farm sizes, diet formulation for stages of life, restructuring production methods, and housing strategies.

Pigs weaned per sow put with a boar changed in the US from around 8 PSY to now many farms weaning 28–33 pigs per sow per year. Feed conversions reduced from over 4 lbs to 2.3–2.5 lbs now on 80–100 lbs. heavier live slaughter weights. The previous 30 years (1945–1975) saw virtually no improvement in these areas of live production.

Expose Yourself to Change

On this backdrop of dramatic change, I'd like to share a few thoughts surrounding the leadership that drove much of this change. In 1974, I asked three others interested in improvements in US pork production to join me on a three-week trip to try to learn why Western Europe was so much more productive than the US. The people we met and the practices we witnessed were eye-opening, and I returned determined to waste little time refining and implementing much of what we learned. Throughout my career, I studied the changes in the broiler industry's benchmarks and costs—after all, they were and continue to be a major competitor.

Clear Vision

From that point on, I had a clear vision of how I wanted to lead our business, which at the time was buying 90+% of the pigs we raised from commingled sales barns. This was a dramatic change; however, having actually seen the differences, I was convinced we could close the gap and better utilize our lower-cost feed ingredients. On the trip, I met Ken Woolley, a founder and President of PIC Worldwide. Later, we decided to work together when I joined PIC and eventually led the US business.

Know What Customers Need vs. Want

I learned many things from Ken, but maybe most of all, it was our role to determine what our customers needed in the form of genetic inputs. Great leaders aren't deterred from their clear vision and the mission of delivery. Ultimately, customers are the winners, even though early on their resistance will need to be met with good data and a clear understanding of not only what to do but how to do it. All good leaders know many good ideas will fail if not supported by excellence in execution.

The Value of Real Change

Early in my career, I would often remind people that real change only occurs with a total disgust for the status quo. That statement is unsettling to many; however, there are at least two types of people in charge: those who are placeholders, focused on a low-risk management style hoping to avoid reduced performance—and the type of leader whose vision is clear and who is determined to change the business significantly, knowing some risk will be part of the formula for success.

Big Step Change

While at PIC, I was exposed to the medicated early weaning concept developed by PIC to help salvage valuable nucleus-level genetics by heavily medicating both sows and newborns, then weaning at 5 days and moving the pigs far away from their mothers, a constant source of infection.

After leaving PIC to take on a leadership role at Murphy Farms in NC, I decided to harvest the medicated early weaning concept and translate it to a commercial application. In 1987, we built our first three 3,600-sow farms designed to wean pigs at 3 weeks and then moved the pigs to off-site nurseries—a brand-new concept at the time. We had two experimental farms to help us convince contract growers and bankers of the concept. Today, this model is the standard in the industry.

When I told Wendell Murphy I planned to build three 3,600-sow units, he asked, "Why not just one to see how it works?" I told him three farms would increase our herd 50%, so we must not fail—and the naysayers would have less effect with three farms. Previously, we had two 1,000-sow farms; all the rest of the 17,000 sows were in 250–500 sow herds. A decade later, we had more than 300,000+ sows—all from organic growth.

After the first three large farms were built, we never built a unit smaller thereafter and enjoyed better performance and lower costs. Turning new confidence and knowledge into action creates an environment young, aggressive people look to join. Recruiting was enhanced by our vision for the future.

Better Talent and New Skill Sets

At Murphy's, we had a growth plan of adding 30,000 sows per year of new construction, along with contract growers building the follow-on nursery and finishing space needed. We added 20–25 college graduates each of the first 5 years, as well as adding company veterinarians and nutritionists. But maybe one of the most unique hires in the early 1990s was in-house financial and production analysts to collect and interpret the data, using sophisticated statistics, into insight to guide changes with confidence.

It was a time when too many managers were struggling with pages of spreadsheets vs. charts and graphs—I often referred to it as the "10-second insight." When people see them, the insight is clear. I never spent time trying to make good production people into analysts. Just give them the charts and graphs.

Today, many family-owned pork production companies are very competitive and are utilizing techniques well beyond the early days of this industry transition.

With a variety of personalities, true leaders are obvious to most after a few minutes. It takes all kinds to build a team, but the leader who sees the path and communicates it often, focuses on key roles and timelines, has a big advantage.

I was very fortunate to have three leaders who helped guide me on this career path and am forever grateful for their confidence, trust, and encouragement.

Chapter 5: Leading in Genetics

Dr. Maurice Bichard

Dr. Bichard could be described as the Father of the Modern Pig. While at Cambridge, he began the practice of quantifying the selection of animals based on statistical data. He has been one of the most influential Geneticists in the world since 1962, when PIC was formed, and he used his expertise.

Dr. Bichard is based in Oxfordshire, UK.

Leadership

A successful business probably needs to embrace people with different sorts of leadership.

Some need the capacity to see it as a commercial enterprise—using a variety of resources, bringing them together, and managing them to provide products or services that can be sold so as to provide an adequate return. These are the classic business leaders.

Others may not be motivated by those objectives but are still leaders in the sense that they want to organise their team of people to carry out their allotted or chosen function efficiently:

- as decided/requested
- on time/consistently
- at reasonable cost in terms of staff, facilities, materials, and time

Still, others may want to *lead* in the sense of promoting new ways of doing things, thus allowing objectives to be reached more quickly, reliably, or cheaply.

I suppose that any leadership that I gave came under this third category. Its origin came from my upbringing, experiences, training, and the opportunities which I chose to grasp.

My Development

I showed a strong interest in livestock farming from the age of 10, beginning by helping on tiny local dairy farms in Guernsey. From 11 to 17, I kept several dairy goats myself for home use and sales. I was then required to spend a year as a farm student, which I completed on a large modern unit in Kent. There, I saw very different methods of producing milk and lamb.

I was at university in the mid-1950s, studying general agriculture at a time when many new scientific disciplines were being promoted as having promise for raising farm output. During vacations, I worked on five more livestock farms, from southern England to the Scottish Borders—three of these belonging to research organisations.

I was increasingly attracted by the application of the new science of quantitative genetics to livestock improvement following its initial successes with selection applied to maize and poultry in the USA. So, I then pursued postgraduate studies, which led to a teaching and research position (1960) in a British university department with a heavy emphasis on these new methods in poultry and pigs. This soon allowed me to have a valuable postdoctoral year in the USA to learn more about genetics and statistics. I was able to meet many of the original academics who had pioneered these methods with livestock over there from the 1930s.

Several animal scientists, particularly in Edinburgh, had confirmed how the pedigreed sectors of farm livestock were traditionally organised into hierarchies, where a small number of herds or flocks were dominant in each breed. Yet in 1960, the owners of these units were unaware of the new data-based methods of selection, and most were not even basing their selection decisions on records of animal performance. In fact, there was active opposition to the adoption of new methods.

The Objective

My aim was, therefore, to help bring about this transformation and thus improve the efficiency of UK livestock production. I chose to try to achieve change in a number of ways.

The Methods

A) Through my teaching of undergraduate and graduate students in my capacity as a university lecturer and supervisor.

B) Academic research into the theory of dissemination of genetic progress within livestock pyramids, leading to published papers in scientific journals and at conferences.

C) Organising pilot demonstration projects using university and college herds and flocks.

D) Membership of national committees that produce reports for farmer and breeder consumption.

E) Membership of national boards responsible for organising new livestock improvement schemes (for example, the Pig Industry Development Authority Nucleus Herd Scheme).

F) Talks to farmer groups.

G) Consultancy with individual breeders or groups who were dissatisfied with existing breeders or official schemes.

In almost all of these activities, I saw myself as a bridge between the more theoretical geneticists and statisticians and the livestock industries—both breeders and commercial producers.

After some 13 years in this university position, I turned down the opportunity to head the breeding programme of one of the UK's leading poultry breeding companies and instead moved (1974) to full-time employment within the pig breeding company whose consultant I had been for the previous eight years. I remained there for another 21 years before retiring. I then worked part-time as a consultant, mainly in the dairy cow sector.

Successes

Looking back over the past 65 years, which of these seven methods has proved effective in advancing the adoption of new scientific methods for livestock improvement? I am thinking not just of my own efforts but those of others engaged in this range of activities.

A) Undergraduate Education

I suspect that very little change has occurred through this channel, certainly in the UK. Most agricultural students at colleges or universities will not be exposed to much genetics or statistics.

Few such institutions have employed lecturers with even my level of training and experience in their application to livestock breeding. Edinburgh, with both its university and the Scottish Agricultural College, has been the one specialist centre backed up by several research units over the decades.

B) Academic studies

My clarification of the factors controlling the flow of genetic change down the multiplication pyramid was certainly used by all major livestock improvement programmes as they became controlled by staff with genetic training.

C) Pilot demonstrations

Our early work with these had no impact on the future practices of UK sheep breeders but may have helped change attitudes away from progeny testing and toward performance testing of boars among pig breeders.

D and E) National committee work

My early work in these roles will have helped make more people throughout the livestock industry aware of the potential impacts of harnessing statistical methods. However, national programmes did not prove to be long-lasting in Britain's poultry or pigs. The situation has been even worse with beef cattle and sheep, where traditional breed societies continue to play a major role in spite of the availability of national recording programmes. Live animal shows still promote judging of individuals on appearance, and the influential breeders are mainly those who succeed in these events.

F) Talks to groups of farmers

Live talks to potential or actual customers have undoubtedly had major impacts on persuading many to try or remain committed to modern breeding programmes. Equally, talking to sales teams has helped them in their understanding and, hence, their ability to win, maintain, and service customers. The requirements here have been the ability to gauge the level of audience knowledge, to prepare thoroughly, and to use language that can be understood. I have frequently been commended by non-English speakers because they could understand my clear diction and vocabulary.

G) Consultancy

Detailed consultancy with potential or actual ongoing clients has surely been a major success in achieving my original goal of persuading livestock industries to utilise the scientific developments continuously produced by academic researchers.

Helping a pig breeding company—originally a group of pig farmers—over 31 years from 1966 to 1995, to create a global business (now a major part of GENUS plc and ranked first in the world as it provides 16% of the breeding stock in the top pig-producing countries) has to be my major contribution.

My initial aim to modernise the UK sheep breeding industry did not achieve success, and I have had no involvement since 1973. The much greater difficulty of performance recording grazing sheep and beef cattle on commercial farms and the range of environmental conditions have made it difficult for improved genetics to be demonstrated there. The major moves so far have been simple changes of breeds, though a few more promising trends can now be detected—after 60 years!

Dairy cattle breeding began to be modernised within farmer cooperatives, which provided both artificial insemination and milk recording services to members. Thus, commercial herds automatically received the benefits of new selection methods. Some of these co-ops evolved into investor-owned companies. GENUS, for example, has been able to adopt methods pioneered in the pig sector for the benefit of both its dairy and beef customers.

The spin-off from my success with pigs eventually led to some other opportunities to help in at least two special situations with dairy cattle. The owners of the farms on the islands of Guernsey and Jersey both face unique problems. They each must continue to keep their own historic breeds and efficiently provide sufficient liquid milk for residents. Over more than 20 years, we have together devised separate improvement programmes which have been adopted by all the herds and are utilising modern technology to make good annual progress while satisfying consumer wishes.

Reflection

On reflection, I believe that there has been one other important component that contributed to my success in getting changes adopted: building a reputation for competence and integrity outside of one's narrow field of employment can pay dividends.

You first have to overcome any reticence to join organisations, learn to speak your mind, and accept increasing responsibilities.

As an undergraduate at the University of Reading, I became an active member of the Agricultural Club and progressed to become Chairman in my final year, thus learning to interact with visiting speakers who were prominent members of the industry. Many years later, I was asked back for a term as President.

As a young lecturer/researcher, I joined a group where academics and the newly emerging poultry breeding companies organised an annual workshop: the Poultry Breeders Roundtable. I eventually served a term as Chairman in the late 1960s.

I joined the British Society of Animal Science as soon as I graduated in 1958, was asked to edit its annual Proceedings during the 1970s, and eventually served as President for 1989/90. I then had four years as Chairman of the organising committee for the European Association for Animal Production's Annual Meeting held in Edinburgh in 1994. I spent many years as a UK delegate to these EAAP annual meetings, serving as Vice President for several years around 1997.

After retirement, when working in the dairy cow sector, I was elected for a year (2007) as President of a breed society (the English Guernsey Cattle Society) and later (2011–2017) spent six years as President of the British Cattle Breeders Club.

By undertaking such roles in organisations related to one's commercial activities, it is possible to raise the profile of your employer—or your own business—through your contacts and reputation. But of course, you have to be prepared to devote adequate time to them, and do them well.

Chapter 6: Building in collaboration in business

Dr. Doug MacDougald

Dr. MacDougald is one of the founders of Southwest Veterinary Services. Not only is he considered one of the most prominent veterinarians in North America, but he is also well known for his management skills, both as a consultant and in his own herds. Doug lives in Ontario.

Reflections on the Path of Leadership

Doug MacDougald

"Leadership is a choice, not a position".

\- **Stephen Covey**

I have not had leadership thrust upon me, nor have I been particularly driven to lead. I hope that I have chosen to lead in those work, family, and community situations where there was a need.

I reflect here on the personal and career path that led to my co-founding South West Vets, a swine practice in Southwestern Ontario that provides a range of services to about seven million pigs per year. South West Vets partnered with two other livestock practices to form Canadian Livestock Vets (CLV), which provides services to 40% of the Canadian swine industry, 30% of the Canadian beef industry, and poultry and other species.

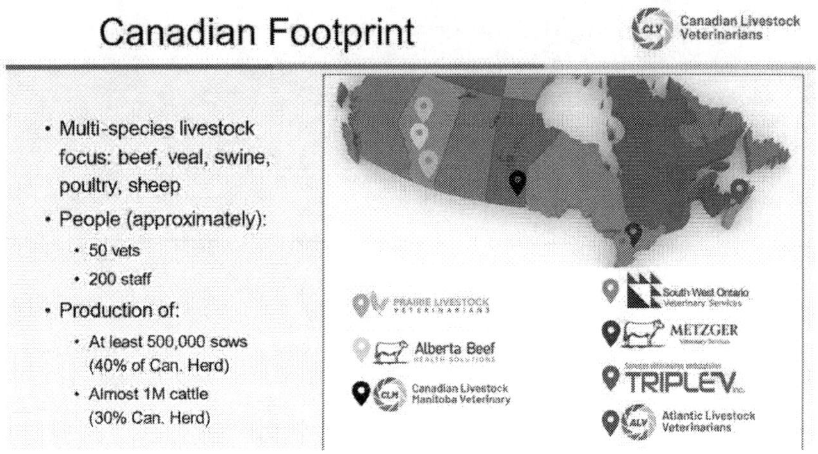

My reflection starts at the beginning—growing up on a swine farm near Fullarton, a hamlet of 60 people in Perth County, and being the second of five children. I attended S.S. 3 Public School in Fullarton, a one-room schoolhouse, until my fifth grade when the baby boomer children led to an expansion to two rooms. I was in a class of five and had the same teacher from grades two to eight. According to my mother, she was not a very good teacher—but there were no worries, as Mom made sure evening studies were up to grade.

I was naïve, introverted, shy, late-maturing (I was the little kid on the end of the girls' row in the Grade 9 class picture for Mitchell District High School), and I grew up with a brother one year older—Bill—who was an extrovert, matured early, and excelled in school and athletics. We were clearly opposites, and I often think now it would have been easy to fold.

However, there was no folding in Walter MacDougald's family. Dad made sure we grew up with strict discipline and accountability for our farm, family, and schoolwork. For example, if any of us got strapped at school, we knew we would get double at home—hey, different era!

We did, however, have the freedom to play and explore without our parents' oversight. They were busy farming and having three more kids after Bill and me. We did all sorts of things that would be viewed as too risky for kids today. Playing tag in the upper level of our empty bank barn, running along the beams 10 feet above the wooden floor, swinging from corner to corner on the centre hayfork rope, or—when it was full of straw bales—pulling the bottom ones out and making a cave inside with no thought of the mow collapsing! I remember a Saturday afternoon with a group of school buddies, probably 12 and 13 years old, getting the bright idea to build a couple of rafts by the Black Creek and float down to where it emptied into the Thames River—at spring flood. What could go wrong other than tipping with rubber boots on? Thankfully, everyone survived, although we were disciplined at home—not for the risk, but for losing the rubber boots! Hey, again, different era. We learned independence and that if you took risks, you were responsible for the outcomes.

My dad was an entrepreneurial pig farmer in the late '50s to the '70s, building a really big finisher barn—40' x 100'—designed to be two levels. He was ahead of his time, setting up contracts and finishing with farmers who were getting out of the dairy business. My brother Bill and I were his labourers, and we learned early the value of work—and a dollar. We had a few pigs of our own when we were young, and we kept a detailed ledger with the full cost for pigs and feed. But I never remember having to pay Dad back the cost difference when the market went south—I guess he wasn't that much of a 'by the book' guy with his kids—but close.

On Saturday mornings, when Bill and I were able to drive, we would go to the farmers who supplied us with feeder pigs, which, of course, back then were weaned at about eight weeks of age. We would early-process the younger piglets for the next pickup, fighting off the sows coming over the partitions as we negotiated with the farmer on the value of the pigs we were buying that day. Our dad gave us a range that was fair, and we had to get the deal done within the 'fair' range—not below or above. As you'll read later in this book, this instilled within us the principle of "win-win," as well as negotiating skills. Great leadership training—I just didn't know it at the time!

There was no competitive hockey for us because Saturdays were farm work days. But we had free rein for high school athletics and other school clubs since they were during or after school, and we would still have time for farm chores.

I had a particularly tough summer turning 16, working at home to paint all the trim on our large brick farmhouse. Who knows if it was finally reaching puberty (finally!) or simply a case of the can't-help-its, but I never did finish the job—and to be honest, this might be the last thing I didn't finish by giving up. My dad, at that point, thought I would never amount to anything, and I decided there wasn't a chance in hell that I would stay home next summer (and yes, by then, I knew the 'other' meaning of hell—outside of Sunday School).

Dad and I had an argument—which I won—when I announced in the fall I was applying to be a Junior Ranger (now the Stewardship Youth Programme) for the next summer. This is an organisation where 17-year-old boys work as a team for the summer with a couple of supervisors, helping maintain—or, in our case, develop—the provincial parks of Ontario. I was placed with a group of 18 guys at Halfway Lake Provincial Park, 80 km north of Sudbury—and we were literally in the middle of the bush as the first team to start building a new park.

I also figured out that most of the boys were from bigger cities, and it was not their choice to be there—rather, their parents were trying to get them away from bad influences. Our foreman, Nels Ojanpera, was a retired mine worker: crusty, blunt, and disciplined. Most of the guys spent the summer bush-whacking out the future roads of the park, which was hot, buggy, and boring.

Because of my farm skills, I ended up leading a small group of four capable guys to build docks, run the chainsaw, build a couple of outbuildings, and do other interesting stuff. Fabulous summer, and I came home having added 10 pounds of muscle, grown up, and confident—Nels taught me how to believe in myself and to be a leader that summer.

As an aside, my most vivid memory of Nels was riding with him in his old Ford pickup truck with the big, long side mirrors. He chewed tobacco, and you couldn't see the driver's side mirror for all the chew spit!

Dad introduced us to—or led us to—business entrepreneurial opportunities. My brother Bill and I had a muskrat trapline in the spring. We had to get up early to check the line, get back home for chores before school, check the trapline after school, do chores, eat supper, and then skin, scrape, and stretch the pelts before schoolwork. Whew—just thinking about our schedule is crazy, but we loved it!

Bill and I bought a new Stihl chainsaw in our late teens in response to the Ontario grant of $500 per farm ($5 per tree) to cut down dead elm trees on fence bottoms and the outside edge of the woodlots. Dutch elm disease caused a blight on the farming landscape in southwest Ontario through the sixties. Ironically, our farm was named Elmsley Farm due to the high number of elm trees on it. We cut down thousands of dead elm trees and learned how to approach (be proactive) and negotiate with farmers (think win-win) on how they could take advantage of this programme, with our help. Great leadership training!

We did this in the summers into our early university years, as well as set up several empty barns to handle feeder pigs. As soon as classes were done, we would go to the Kitchener-Waterloo sales barn and buy hundreds of feeder pigs. One year, we had enough barn space for 700 pigs. We made sure to buy all the ruptures and ridglings because they were inexpensive—and we fixed them. Note: we were taught by Dad to do these surgeries, not vet school!

Every morning, we would get on the road on a 200cc BSA motorcycle and do chores in the different barns, cut elm trees the rest of the day—and then I played fastball for the Fullarton A's at night. Whew! I don't know if this was leadership training, but I learned the value of hard work.

Bill and I bought a house in Guelph in the early '70s and tried to buy another but missed out on it. We never lived there since we could live at a lower cost with our buddies—usually in a 'beater' house. It was a successful rental property, purchased for $17,000 in 1973 and sold for $28,000 in 1977. Did we ever think we were smart? Yeah, right—looking back, we should have bought 12 and kept them! Although with inflation peaking at 21% in 1981, that might have rocked our world a bit.

All these stories lead to: **"Thanks, Dad."**

As an aside, however, Dad had no use for veterinarians. He had one on the farm once, and the pig died, and Dad became "Dr. MacDougald" after that. When I was accepted into vet school, Dad's quote to a community friend was, *"Well, that will be a waste of skin."* Dad rarely changed his opinion—but on this one, he did. Eventually.

I was lucky, as the aforementioned naïve, introverted, shy, and late-maturing kid, to eventually have considerable success in school and athletics. Sports have been a very important part of my leadership training—even though, at the time, I didn't know it. We were just having fun.

I have had a few important role models in my life, and two were involved in sports. Dave Service was a newly graduated Phys Ed teacher when I started to make high school teams in Grade 11 or 12, and he led our group of 'jocks' to some athletic successes. He showed us his approach of leading by example—participating in drills, scrimmages, and workouts. This made a lasting impression on me. A tight group of guys competing together, led by an excellent role model, taught me the importance of teamwork, communication, sharing, and mutual support. Even if I didn't know it at the time, this was valuable leadership training.

Five years of varsity rugby at Guelph cemented these values for me. My second role model was our coach, John Keegan, a former professional rugby player from New Zealand. John was another lead-by-example coach. He was always on the field, and at the end of grueling practices, he led us on a sprint around the playing field. He made it clear that by the end of the season, he expected someone to beat him. Most didn't—but a couple did. I wasn't one of them—but boy, did I try hard.

In the five years of playing varsity, we won two Ontario University Athletic Association championships—one B level and one A level. I was captain and MVP for two years, not as a gifted natural athlete but through 110% effort, working to keep from letting my teammates or coaches down. However, I did learn that winning was a nice culture to have! This was the best leadership training—and again, I didn't know it. We were just having fun. Our 1974 team was inducted into the University of Guelph Gryphons Hall of Fame—what an honour.

Ten years into my career as a private-practicing large animal veterinarian and one of four partners in the Milverton-Wellesley Vet Clinic—a traditional mixed-animal practice—I developed a vision of a different business model for agricultural veterinary medicine. The idea was to specialise in swine with a focus on production, management, and herd health, with insights from production and financial information (see the Alvin Toffler reference later in this chapter). My partners didn't support this vision, so—being young (35), confident (some might have said cockily), and recently divorced, supporting my family, and living in a rented country bungalow for $150/month—I left my secure partnership and set up a swine practice in the mudroom and garage of my house.

What could go wrong?

Lots could have gone wrong—but it was highly successful. I was no longer the shy, introverted kid. In addition to the above business vision, I started my practice with some different ends in mind. One of those, as a separated dad of two young boys, was having enough time to be an important part of their lives. The traditional vet partnership I was in did not allow, in my opinion, enough flexibility or time away from work. (See Covey's 7th Habit—*Sharpen the Saw*—below.)

In addition to childhood, sports, and entrepreneurial experiences, leadership growth for me has come through authors, with critical and timely books that have shaped my life.

Alvin Toffler was an American writer and futurist. His trilogy had a meaningful impact on me and changed how I viewed change, opportunity, and the future—as well as my thinking on the veterinary business model.

- *Future Shock* (1970): focused on the changing technology and societal impact of the time
- *Third Wave* (1980): focused on the emerging trends of personal computers, internet, cable, and mobile communication
- *Power Shift* (1990): spoke to the power of knowledge, wealth, and influence—with a shift into a knowledge-based society.

The most important mentorship author in my life has been Stephen Covey, the author of *The 7 Habits of Highly Effective People* (1989). This, and two of his other books—*Principle-Centred Leadership* (1992) and *First Things First* (1996)—have been the most frequent gifts I've given to my children, nephews, nieces, friends, and colleagues. Often, I included the inscription: *"I wish I had read and understood these Seven Habits at your age."*

The book is laid out through seven habits, with the first three aimed at achieving private victories or independence, the next three as a means of achieving public victories or interdependence, and the final habit as a means to renew yourself.

The 7 Habits

Be proactive

Proactive people take responsibility for events, challenges, and opportunities that are within their circle of influence. They spend no time or resources on things within a much bigger circle of concern over which they have no influence.

Begin with the end in mind.

This habit means clarifying your goals and values to guide your actions. It includes creating a mission statement, defining your principles, and asking, "How do I want to feel at the end of the day, month, year, or life?" On a practical basis, it's about defining the targeted outcome of a project, change, strategy, or vision.

Put first things first.

This habit is the execution of the first two habits. With discipline, determine important tasks and execute them effectively:

1. Prioritise Quadrant 1: urgent and important tasks
2. Plan Quadrant 2: not urgent but important tasks
3. Delegate Quadrant 3: urgent but not important tasks
4. Eliminate Quadrant 4: not urgent and not important tasks

(*Source: Wikipedia*)

Think win-win

Seek mutually beneficial solutions in your relationships. Embrace an abundance mentality—the belief that there is more than enough for everybody, as well as opportunity for growth. This comes from being open-minded, creative, flexible, collaborative, and cooperative. The opposite is a scarcity mentality, where one person's success must come at another's loss, thus limiting opportunities.

Personal note: see the earlier reference to my dad setting the feeder pig 'to be negotiated' value with a fair or win-win price—early lessons for a teenager.

Seek first to understand, then to be understood.

Use active and empathetic listening to genuinely understand someone. This means listening with the intent to understand, not to respond! It creates an atmosphere of caring and positive problem-solving.

Synergise

Combine the strengths of people through positive collaboration to achieve goals that no one could have accomplished alone. This creates outcomes greater than the sum of the parts.

Sharpen the saw

Balance and renew your resources, energy, and health to create a long-term, effective lifestyle. Focus on physical, mental, emotional, and spiritual renewal.

Embracing Covey's *Seven Habits* created a structure or playbook for my life. Achieving *independence* or personal victories through the first three habits—be proactive, begin with the end in mind, and put first things first—is brilliant in its simplicity and amazingly effective when applied to internal goals.

Achieving *interdependence* or public victories through the next three habits—think to win-win, listen to understand before being understood, synergise—has been my external blueprint to follow.

And *sharpening the saw* has simply given me a more fulfilling and purposeful life.

My entire career has been one of collaboration, partnerships, and believing that the *outcome is greater than the sum of the parts*. This mindset has led me to become a partner in more than 20 companies—including veterinary practices, real estate, agricultural businesses with clients, investments, and more. None of this was done alone.

At no time were these habits more valuable than when we formed South West Vets. Through the 1990s and into the 2000s, there were six veterinary practices in southwest Ontario primarily focused on the swine industry. Each had one or two veterinarians, and in the small 150 km x 150 km geographic footprint where most of the industry operated, these vets would literally drive past each other on their way to clients.

From an efficient business model perspective, this made absolutely no sense—nor did it if we applied Covey's 6th habit, *synergise*.

It became apparent there was a great opportunity to create a different and better business model. Dr Marty Misener was a veterinarian in one of the six practices—we had known and respected each other for decades. Through co-leading the Ontario Swine Health Advisory Board starting in 2005, we became close friends and colleagues. With Marty's leadership, we called the six practices to a meeting in late 2006 and pitched a merger plan.

This led to a joint pharmacy enterprise in 2007, while the individual practices continued to operate professionally as they were. This could easily have remained a "buying group" model—but Marty and I were adamant this added little value. Only through a full merger into a single practice would we achieve value for ourselves, our clients, and our industry through the synergistic power of working together as one.

South West Vets was formed in 2010 and remains one of the highlights of my business career. We had to foster this vision over many years, working through the challenge of leaving six cultures behind to form a new culture and brand. I have been blessed to have helped form and lead South West Vets through most of the last 20 years of my career. Thank you, Covey—and thank you, Marty.

I have often said, *"I was born with reasonably high IQ (thank you,* Mom *and Dad), but with ZERO emotional intelligence."*

Emotional intelligence (EI), also known as emotional quotient (EQ), is the ability to perceive, use, understand, manage, and handle emotions. High emotional intelligence includes recognising emotions in yourself and others, using emotional information to guide thinking and behaviour, discerning and labelling different feelings, and adjusting emotions to adapt to environments. (*Source: Wikipedia*)

As I read more and reflected through various personal and professional challenges and failures—as well as living with my wife Barbara, who has abundant EQ—it became clear I needed to figure this out.

Covey's books helped, but a swine vet conference in Quebec in 1997 was a *light bulb moment* for me. It included a half-day session on communications and an introductory course on the Myers-Briggs Type Indicator. Notwithstanding some questions on the scientific validity of the results, it defines people through a 120-question questionnaire as one of 16 primary personality types, with various strengths and weaknesses.

My wife Barbara, after reading the description of my type, said: *"How can 120 questions be so accurate about who you are, Doug?"* After seeking more information through reading, counselling, and coaching, I was truly able to begin applying Covey's 5th habit: *seek first to understand before being understood* (*For those interested, my type is INTJ.*).

Personal note to reader: as Barbara, Marty, and others will know, I am a work in progress—often better, but not always.

A little aside from that Quebec conference in 1997, continuing the theme of collaborative leadership, a group of Canadian swine veterinarians created the Canadian Swine Forum. This was a newsletter for our clients and industry, and we maintained publication for years. For a group of competitors, we had an amazingly collaborative culture.

Viktor Frankl's 1946 book, *Man's Search for Meaning*, is one I have read several times—often at a time when I needed a personal reset after a challenge or failure. The first half of the book chronicles Frankl's experiences in Nazi concentration camps during World War II. The second half describes logotherapy—a search for life's meaning or purpose as the central human motivational force. Frankl developed the concept of logotherapy during the years he spent in concentration camps.

This is a book with a very powerful leadership message on a very personal level, and for me, it was—and is—an example of *sharpening the saw*.

Part of the 7th habit is service to society, and I had my Mom and Dad as role models, as they, for their lifetime, supported their communities.

It wasn't until over 20 years ago, during a personal retreat at Lake Louise—skiing alone for five days and spending evenings with my books and thoughts—that I planned the next stage of my life. That plan included increasing my community service, as well as beginning some type of international service.

Community service included organisations whose causes were meaningful and impactful. International service came through *Sleeping Children Around the World* (www.scaw.org), a wonderful small Canadian charity helping some of the poorest children in the world. This has taken me, in a leadership role, to several countries in South Asia and Africa over the last 18 years.

Through those five days on retreat, I wrote a mission statement, as well as the roles and principles under which I wished to live. I include this below, even though it is very personal. We all have different aspirations, and I would encourage everyone to go through this personal reflection and planning process.

Are mine hard to do? Absolutely.

Am I always successful? Never.

But a lifetime of aspiring for excellence means, for me, a purposeful life—learning from my mistakes and trying to live with no regrets.

Mission Statement

I will focus on consistent improvement of my spiritual, emotional, mental, and physical well-being, so that I may contribute to excellence with my family, work, community, and self.

Roles

Family

- Husband
- Dad, “Papa”
- Son, Brother, Uncle, etc.

Work

- Veterinarian

- Business Manager / Leader
- Partner
- Mentor
- Colleague
- Industry Leader

Community

- Stratford Perth Community Foundation
- Clan MacDougald
- Sleeping Children
- Other Services / Charities
    - Time
    - Talent
    - Treasure

Personal

- Fitness / Athlete
- Lifelong Learner Traveller
- Friend
- Investor

Principles

- Integrity
- *The 7 Habits:*
  - Be Proactive
  - Begin with the End in Mind
  - Put First Things First
  - Think "Win–Win"
  - Seek First to Understand, Then to Be Understood Synergise
  - Sharpen the Saw
- Excellence Is a Choice

Biography

Doug MacDougald, DVM, has been a veterinarian for over 47 years, retiring as a partner in 2024 from South West Ontario Veterinary Services—an Ontario practice with a swine health, production, diagnostic, and information focus—and from Canadian Livestock Veterinarians, a national practice with beef, poultry, and swine services in eight provinces.

Doug and his wife, Barbara, have four children and nine grandchildren. In addition to his family and professional responsibilities, Doug has served in various community and industry organisations with time, talent, and treasure.

He also organises *Clan MacDougald*, a family dragon boat team that has, for twenty-four years, supported the Stratford Rotary Dragon Boat Festival. He is a travelling volunteer with *Sleeping Children Around the World*, a Canadian charity that helps the poorest children in the world.

Doug has received numerous awards and recognitions, including:

- The **2011 YMCA Peace Medal** for international humanitarian work
- The **2015 Ontario Veterinary Medical Association Outstanding Veterinarian of the Year Award**

- The **2015 Canadian Veterinary Medical Association / Merck Veterinary Award** for the advancement of large animal medicine and herd health management
- In 2020, he was named a **Paul Harris Fellow** by the Rotary Club of Stratford.

Bill and I went to the barn at a young age.

Dad, Bill and me

Bill and me with muskrat pelts

Dad & Mom with from left, Bill, Doug, Jan, Patricia, and Ormond at our parents' 50th anniversary with an endowed scholarship in their name.

ACADEMIC
GLEE CLUB
BASKETBALL
SOCCER
EXECUTIVE
PREFECT
SERVICE
JR. DRAMA
FOOTBALL
SR. DRAMA
ATHLETICS
CROSS COUNTRY

High School

U. of G. Rugby OUAA champions 1974. Doug, back row, second from left.

A Sleeping Children trip to Tanzania – bubbles and kids – doesn't get better.

Our family 2023

Chapter 7: Revitalizing a rural community

Kim McConnell

Kim founded and runs AdFarm, a highly successful advertising company that serves the agriculture industry. Kim has also been on multiple boards and is one of the most respected people in Canada in terms of agriculture. Kim is based in Calgary, Canada.

Revitalizing a Rural Community

Every summer, I enjoy returning to my hometown in rural Manitoba to visit family and friends and spend time on the farm. This summer, I added another item to the summer siesta—along with a couple of community leaders, we initiated an exercise to help revitalise our town of 850 residents, located one hour from a regional city and 200 miles from a major city.

The journey started with a casual discussion with a friend who is also the CEO of the local credit union. We lamented the demise of rural communities and our desire to revitalise our little town. The conversation began by admitting that our community wasn't overly special. While we are in a prime agricultural area, we're located on a secondary highway, have no rail line, and no major businesses beyond a few retail stores. We have good schools and wonderful sports and lifestyle facilities, a health clinic, a small hospital, and an overcrowded personal care home. But we have one unique feature: we have six (6) doctors!

More than one doctor is an anomaly in most rural areas, and with this unique feature, we wondered what we could do to stimulate enthusiasm in the community. Our first step was to discuss the opportunity with a good friend and respected community leader. The three of us put together some basic thoughts. We then invited five other community leaders to join us for a discussion. We outlined our initial ideas—and these people got excited. A few days later, we held another meeting that attracted 28 people. Again, we presented our thoughts and ideas.

We opened the meeting by suggesting that we believed our "six-doctor situation" provided a unique opportunity. We asked why we couldn't expand and deliver 24-hour emergency health care service. We learned that a key reason was the lack of lab and x-ray technicians. We discussed how we could overcome this challenge. One of the participants, a former doctor, said, *"I think I might be able to help solve this issue."* Someone else added, *"I'd like to help you."* So, we set up the foundation for a **Health Care Committee**.

We then discussed another hurdle facing the community—housing. There were no houses or apartments available to buy or rent. A young man who is also a carpenter said, *"I don't have any money, but I'd like to see how I might be able to overcome this challenge."* Another participant said, *"I'd like to help you with that,"* so we set up a **Building Committee**.

We all agreed that the lifestyle our little community offers is very good and that a key to a strong community is ensuring that the lifestyle activities and all the facilities remain attractive. To do this, we set up the foundation for a **Lifestyle Committee**.

Some said, *"We're going to need some money to get things going."* Everyone agreed that attracting money shouldn't be a problem, but we needed a plan. A new resident to the community jumped in and said, *"I have a background in fund development, and I'd like to see what I can do to pull a plan together and seek out possible funding programmes."* An accountant raised her hand and said, *"I'll help you with that."* So, we set up a **Fund Development Committee**.

Then, we agreed that we needed an **Executive Committee** to pull all the committees and their activities together. This, too, was established that evening, with a respected community leader stepping forward to become the Chair. The Mayor also joined the executive committee, along with spots for each of the committee chairs. The following week, the Executive Committee met and hired a part-time general manager to work with each of the committees and advance their work.

All this occurred in a five-week period. And while the results will take some time to materialise, the town is buzzing. In fact, an open community meeting was held a few weeks later to update the residents—and over 10% of the entire population was in attendance.

Today, this little rural community is alive with energy. And something else is happening. Many younger people have stepped forward and are involved in the committees. So are members of the growing Filipino community, who have relocated to the area and are making this community their home. It's an exciting time.

So, what lessons can be shared that might be of value to other communities? Here are a few:

1. **Determine your unique value proposition**. What is the feature your community offers that makes it unique and something you can build upon? Ours was *"six doctors."*

2. **Start small.** Begin with a small group of three people. Get together and come up with a basic plan to overcome the challenge and/or deliver on the opportunity.

3. **Write it down** Write down your thoughts so that they can be easily shared. Make this plan short and simple—and *don't* make it look too good.

4. **Share the plan.** Share your very simple thoughts and ask others for their input and recommendations for improvement.

   Note: If the plan is basic and doesn't look too finished, then participants are more likely to offer ideas for improvement—and they are much more likely to get engaged.

Remember: Involvement = Engagement.

5. **Improve the plan and share it with others.** Expand the circle of involvement. And keep expanding the circle and improving the plan.

6. **Make things fun.** Ensure the meetings are enjoyable and that progress advances.

Revitalising rural communities and building strong businesses have many similarities. Success involves leadership, a plan, and making things happen.

Enjoy the journey.

Kim McConnell, CM

Chapter 8: The Disrupter speaks

Mark Greenwood

Mark Greenwood is a true disruptor. He revolutionized the way the banking industry assesses and services Agriculture, especially pig farming. He made it his and Compeer's goal to understand the business of pig farming and to assess producers' risk management strategies. No one else has done this before.

Mark lives with his family in Minnesota.

Life is a Journey

Most people will have leadership responsibility at some point in their life. Whether you are a parent with children or leading a department in an organisation, you will have an opportunity to lead in some capacity. I have learned throughout my life journey that it is not about the title you receive, but what you do through your actions that makes a difference as a leader. I have tried to focus my life on **servant leadership**—you put others first instead of yourself. Throughout this chapter, I will go over points that helped me along the way, and I hope they will help you.

A Solid Foundation: I was lucky to have two incredible parents who were great role models. My father, Ike, was a farmer, and my mother, Helen, was a teacher. They did not hold big positions with large organisations, but how they served throughout their lives gave me a solid foundation. In my opinion, they lived lives well lived.

My father passed away from cancer in the early 1980s when I was twenty-three years old. One of the hardest things I have ever done was talking to Dad about his funeral wishes. He was more concerned about my mom and me as we discussed his funeral. When he was dealing with cancer, he was taking experimental treatments. He had to sign a waiver acknowledging that these treatments were high-risk and could potentially shorten his life. The reason he did this was the hope it would help others in the future. He was selfless. I still have a copy of the personal letter from the doctor at Mayo Clinic thanking my father for his willingness to participate in clinical research trials. Throughout his life, he always put others first—which is foundational to being a good leader.

My mother went back to school to earn her bachelor's degree in her late forties. She was the oldest person in her class by over 20 years. Her first job was to teach children with special needs in the 1960s in my hometown. She had a gift for maximising students' talents and getting the most out of their abilities. As leaders, we need to be lifelong learners at any age, and in leading a team of people, we need to maximise their talents to find success. I had a great foundation from an early age as to what it takes to be successful in life—and that came from my parents.

Unwavering Support and Sacrifice: Leadership can be lonely at times. I was incredibly lucky to be married to my best friend and supporter, Beth. There were countless days when I questioned myself, my abilities, and the decisions I made. She listened and supported me. There were endless days when I was travelling, and she oversaw taking care of our family. She made numerous sacrifices so I could do my job to the best of my ability. She was also the one encouraging me to take on new challenges that I genuinely believe I would not have pursued without her support and encouragement. Leadership takes people who stand beside you and support you through good and tough times.

Other People Need to Give You That Opportunity: I was fortunate throughout my life that other leaders gave me opportunities. They didn't know for sure whether I would be effective—they took a chance on me. Many of the people who gave me those chances became mentors.

It's About Them, Not You: In writing this chapter, I did a lot of self-reflection about what I've learned along the way. In my early 30s, I took a position as a Regional Sales Manager for an animal nutrition company. I thought I was ready to lead people—and I was excited to have a title that went with the role. I was more concerned about my status than about effectively managing a team. I also thought in that first supervisory role, I had to show the team that I knew more than they did.

Managing or leading people is about helping them become the best version of themselves. Every person is unique. We need to focus on what we can do to support them in their roles—not on how we can look better to our boss or colleagues.

Leading as an Individual Contributor: After about eight years as a sales team leader, I switched careers and became a loan officer for the Farm Credit system. I'm sure people around me were wondering what a former feed rep was doing as a loan officer. However, the experience of cold-calling, leading a sales team, and understanding farmers—especially livestock farmers—proved invaluable in relating to clients.

During the late 1990s and early 2000s, there was tremendous growth in the swine industry. I was fortunate to help people grow their businesses through acquisition or greenfield expansion. My earlier career experience helped me communicate what worked and what didn't. I earned trust, and many clients grew and prospered during that time. Though I wasn't leading a team, I was leading clients—helping them grow their business.

I didn't supervise anyone during this period, but I helped shape a segment of agriculture. I learned a great deal from individual owners and large corporations. Helping them grow and observing what succeeded or failed gave me a broader perspective on supporting people in their journeys. Sometimes, it happened in a boardroom; often, it was across a kitchen table. Each interaction was a chance to help someone improve their business—or, when things weren't going well, have the difficult conversations. This experience shaped how I grew as a leader.

Talk Less – Listen More: This is still hard for me, even now that I'm semi-retired. It is so important to truly listen to what people are saying so you can understand their point of view. Too often, we jump to the conclusion that we already know the best solution—without taking the time to understand the other person's perspective.

It's hard to lead someone if they don't believe they're being heard. If they feel unheard, they'll lose trust in you—quickly. In our world today, listening is becoming a lost art. We tend to interrupt or talk over people before they've finished expressing themselves.

Talk less—listen more.

Humility Is Way More Important Than Any Title: I learned this the hard way early in my career. When I was having remarkable success at Farm Credit, I thought I could fix anyone's situation if I became their lender. After some reflection, I realised I was so naïve. I had a couple of situations that did not go well, and it cost our organisation. There are so many factors you cannot control, and sometimes, the risks you take do not work out. You want to blame the people you were involved with—but you also need to look in the mirror.

Humility makes you realise that you never have everything figured out and there are limits to what you can control. If you have been given leadership responsibility, remember what got you into that position. Yes, it was your talents—but it was also the people you surround yourself with. They enable you to be a good leader.

Hire people who have the potential to be better than you. Appreciate what they do, and always show them gratitude. I had a habit, as a leader, of walking through any office I was in. I tried to say hello and get to know people's names and roles. Yes, it gets harder when you lead a larger organisation—but you still need to take time to make a connection with employees, regardless of their position. It goes a long way in establishing a healthy organisational culture.

The knowledge I gained by doing those walk-throughs gave me a better overall understanding of the organisation.

Being Consistent: How many of you like a leader when you don't know how they will react in a crisis? Being reliable, knowledgeable, and supportive during times of uncertainty is extremely important.

In 2020, we faced COVID—a situation none of us had ever experienced. People were wondering how we were going to act as leaders and how we would respond as a financial services company. We did our best to communicate—but more importantly, we were consistent with our messaging.

Giving people assurances during great times of uncertainty is especially important as a leader.

Handling Crucial Conversations: Throughout your life, you will have crucial—or difficult—conversations. This could be with a client, a direct report, a team you're coaching, or even your supervisor. There are times you would love to avoid the conversation, but eventually, you'll need to have it.

Here are a few items to consider when faced with this:

- **First**, put your thoughts in writing so you are clear on the points you need to address.
- **Second**, never conduct a crucial conversation via email. The best practice is face-to-face. If you're in a virtual setting, make sure you can see each other. Reading facial expressions matters.
- **Third**, stay calm. Keep your emotions in check. I've made the mistake of losing my composure—and in doing so, lost the point I was trying to make.

Ask for understanding. Do they fully grasp the points you're addressing? Do they need clarification?

Once you've shared your view, the next part is critical: **listen to theirs**. You owe that person the opportunity to explain their perspective. Maybe it was a misunderstanding. Maybe something needed to be clarified.

Regardless of the situation, they need to feel heard.

The final piece of any crucial conversation is defining your expected outcome. If your goal is simply to prove you're right—

you're wrong. The goal is to gain understanding and develop a plan with clear next steps. Maybe that includes benchmarks or a follow-up check-in. Maybe they didn't fully understand the expectations in the first place.

Either way—you need to have the conversation.

Being OK With Being Uncomfortable: There was never a time in my career when discomfort didn't lead to growth. Yes, sometimes the outcomes weren't ideal—but I learned from those situations.

There were times I was asked to do things I wasn't sure I could do. I told people we were going to aim for goals that felt unachievable. And we tried.

I had leaders who pushed me—sometimes to levels that felt unrealistic—but in doing so, they also pushed me beyond what I thought was possible. If you've ever set a goal and then realised it was too easy, did you think *I should've set the bar higher*? The answer should be yes.

Even if you don't reach a far-reaching goal, it's more rewarding to stretch than to settle.

Push yourself. Be willing to be uncomfortable in the pursuit of growth.

<u>Having a Circle of Trusted Advisors:</u> Throughout my career and life, I always had people I could go to for input—people I trusted to bounce around ideas. As a leader, you need people to talk to when facing complex or sensitive issues.

It's important to develop a circle of people you can confide in—who won't judge you and who will listen with honesty and clarity. This circle should be willing to offer **brutally honest feedback**, even when you don't want to hear it. It's how you grow.

Your circle of advisors will (and should) change throughout your life. Another key element? Confidentiality. Leadership can be a lonely place if you don't have someone to talk to. I've learned that first-hand.

<u>Building a Team and Having a Solid Bench:</u> Hiring and assembling an excellent group of people is vital to a successful organisation. Having a team of leaders with a mindset of continuous improvement, resistance to complacency, and a willingness to provide honest feedback significantly enhances your chances of success.

If you're building a team, bring in people with **different talents** who all focus on what's best for the organisation—not themselves.

If someone is more concerned about "I" than "we," they may succeed in the short term—but not in the long term.

Take basketball as an example. You might have a top scorer—but you also need defenders, rebounders, and playmakers. Every role matters.

Understanding the importance of **people and the roles they play** in the success of the organisation is crucial.

The More Responsibility You Have, the More Important It Is to Widen Your Lens: When you have greater responsibility for the direction of the organisation, it is imperative to keep your head up and not get lost in the details of every department. You need to understand what is happening across the organisation and rely on the leaders of those departments to do their jobs well.

You also need to appreciate how each department contributes to the broader goals. It is your role to **encourage collaboration** and to reinforce that each area is vital to the organisation's success.

People will watch closely to see whether you show favouritism. Be sure to **recognise all employees** for their part in the organisation's success.

The Greater Your Responsibility, the More You Are Being Watched: In today's world of mobile phones and the ability to capture any situation on video, it is imperative to be aware of how your actions are perceived. I've seen people ruin their careers based on poor behaviour at a dinner reception, during a leadership meeting, or in interactions with former peers who are now subordinates.

Not everyone may be your biggest supporter—and some may be waiting for a moment of weakness to hold against you. It's an unfortunate reality but one that requires constant awareness.

People notice and follow good leadership. **You are always being watched.**

Daily Habits That Make You a Better Leader—But More Importantly, a Better Person: I've adopted a set of daily habits that have made me a better leader and, more importantly, a better person.

- **Start each day with a thought of gratitude.** Every day is a gift. Take a couple of minutes to thank God for the opportunities you've been given. Starting your day with gratitude will shift your outlook—for the better.
- **Work on your body as well as your mind** I started this habit in my late 20s. I would either go for a run or a walk. It gave me time to clear my head and physically prepare for the day. Many of my best ideas came while I was moving.
- **Keep your priorities in order** Faith, family, and work—this should be your priority order. I didn't always get this right, but the older I became, the more I realised that honouring

these priorities made me a better person and a better leader. It brings authenticity and clarity to what truly matters.

- **Take time for silence.** In a world of constant connection and 24/7 access, taking time for silence is vital. It helps clear your mind and sets your focus for the day.
- **Be a lifelong learner.** I try to learn something new every day—whether through a book, a podcast, or a coffee chat with a friend. The opportunities are endless if you're open to them.
- **Get better every day—don't get complacent.** This is a mindset I've noticed in not just successful people but also happy ones. If you work on being a good person, you will naturally become a better leader. I'm a strong believer in **servant leadership**. We are here to serve others—and it is a beautiful way to live.

Final Thought and Quote

When you reach the age of 65 (yes, that's me), you're entering the fourth quarter of life. There aren't as many years left. The older I get, the deeper my sense of gratitude grows—towards the people I've met along the way.

When I retired, I shared a quote from Matthew Kelly's *The Rhythm of Life*. It sums up my philosophy on leadership and life:

"The people we surround ourselves with either raise or lower our standards.

They either help us to become the best version of ourselves or encourage us to become lesser versions of ourselves.

We become like our friends.

No man becomes great on his own. No woman becomes great on her own.

The people around them help to make them great.

We all need people in our lives who raise our standards, remind us of our essential purpose,

and challenge us to become the best version of ourselves."

—Matthew Kelly, The Rhythm of Life: Living Every Day with Passion and Purpose

I hope there was some value for you in this chapter of the book. **I wish you all the best in your life journey.*—Mark Greenwood***

Chapter 9: Operational Leadership

Dr. Carthy Templeton

Dr. Templeton is a widely respected veterinarian located in Ontario, Canada. She also manages Synergy Swine, a very successful pig production business. She is a pioneer as a woman working in a predominantly male-dominated industry. She also breeds and rides horses.

Hello. My name is Catherine Templeton, and I have been asked by Ben Woolley to share some of my career with you. I am a veterinarian in southwestern Ontario, and I have had some involvement in developing a pork production group called Synergy.

As background, I grew up near a small Quebec community close to the U.S. border. That community was largely English-speaking, but French and English lived in harmony, with considerable cross-connections. Our family—my parents, my sister, my brother, and I—lived with my maternal grandparents on a fruit and beef farm owned and operated by my grandfather, Bob Reid.

Bobby, as we called him, was fundamental in developing my roots in agriculture. He was the local Provincial Agricultural Representative and worked in extension across southern Quebec. He was also a strong leader in our local community, and we had—and still have—strong community ties. My brother and I spent many days and hours with him, going on farm calls that were part of his job and working with him on the farm. I knew from a young age that I wanted to be involved in agriculture.

After high school, I set my sights on attending the University of Guelph. Guelph was a great place—friendly and welcoming, with so many new people and opportunities. Along the way, I completed a B.Sc (Agr) and married my high school sweetheart, Dan Templeton. He was at the Ontario Veterinary College, completed his DVM, and moved on to a mixed practice in Seaforth, Ontario, while I was four years behind him, working toward becoming a veterinarian myself.

I had no background in swine, but I was lucky enough to spend two summers at the Provincial Diagnostic Lab at Huron Park with Drs. Gaylan Josephson and Ernie Sanford. They gave me some knowledge of swine diseases, which proved useful when I graduated and started in mixed practice. At that time, there were few vets interested in swine practice, so even having a little knowledge and interest made it easy for me to be a "big fish in a small pond." It's easy to be an expert in a field with limited competition. I really, really liked the pork producers and found them interesting—more innovative and more open than producers in the supply-managed sectors.

I spent five years in mixed practice, gradually expanding my swine work. During that time, I was fortunate to be given opportunities in swine health and management by Dr. Mike Wilson. Mike, in addition to being a professor at OVC, was one of the first Ontario pork producers to be involved in three-site production. His herd, Cobbity Farms, along with two other Ontario herds, shipped the first weanlings to a start-up company in

Minnesota called New Fashion Pork. It was a huge opportunity to do hands-on learning in pork production.

Another big decision that Dan and I made was to start farming ourselves. Not having the financial resources to go it alone, we approached this with partners. Over a 25-year period, we owned and operated farms through a series of partnerships with other producers. Key to this process was recognising what knowledge and resources we had—and didn't have—and finding partners whose skills complemented ours.

Deciding in advance how things were going to be done and what the exit plan was before entering the partnership was extremely helpful. We were very lucky to have great partners along the way, and we hope that we will be good partners in return. These situations are not a walk in the park. They require patience, persistence, cooperation, and compromise. In the long run, they became positive, long-term relationships that helped fill the gaps in our knowledge or ability—and also created lifelong friendships.

Being a practice owner was one of my goals, and the opportunities for that seemed limited where I was. So, I decided to take the big leap and go out on my own in swine practice. Without a large client base, I began doing some work with an accounting firm involved in swine farms. It was there that I met Bas Haefling, an accountant who helped me understand that there was another dimension to being a successful pork producer: financial management.

Bas was a great mentor. Because of him, I became a strong advocate for solutions that involved financial as well as biological health. Production excellence and good health were only two segments of the production wheel—there was more!

On my own as a swine vet, I was hungry for knowledge about the industry across North America and Europe. I took every opportunity to attend conferences, interact with other young swine vets, and observe production systems wherever I could. I wanted to know what was happening.

What I saw **panicked** me. Something had to be done.

Our Ontario industry was in trouble. Many small farrow-to-finish operations had dubious facilities and pig health. We were falling further and further behind the rest of the North American industry. Worse still, our marketing system—though not supply-managed—was a kind of managed marketing that **impeded progress**.

At the time, Ontario Pork operated a single-desk selling for all market animals in Ontario. Producers called in "lots" of hogs to a central desk, and hogs were sold anonymously by Dutch auction. The Packers had no idea what, or whose, hogs they were bidding on. There was no way for excellence in hog quality to be recognised, and packers were handcuffed in trying to develop production efficiencies since they didn't know what hogs they were receiving.

Others recognised this situation too. As we looked at what producers in other parts of the continent were achieving, we knew something had to change in Ontario.

In 1994, a group of four of us—Ron Coghlin and Mark Youngblut from Molesworth Farm Supply, Bob Fraser (then with NPD Genetics), and myself—spent many hours trying to solve the problems we saw in our world.

In the end, we came together to establish a **vertically coordinated production system**, which we called **Synergy**. This system had to create opportunities along the value chain for all participants. Inherent in the plan was the desire to **preserve communities** and the **land-based family operations** that supported them.

Synergy – The Evolution

From 1993 to 1994, the opportunity for direct contracts between packers and producers began to open up. This gave processors a chance to understand exactly what they were purchasing. If they knew what they were getting—both in terms of numbers and quality—they could increase efficiency. Previously, purchasing by Dutch Auction through Ontario Pork had left them blind to the actual source of the hogs, with huge variability in offerings.

The vision of the Synergy group was to create **win-win situations** for all participants. Producers could work together to supply a predictable weekly number of hogs of superior quality—through consistent feed, health, and genetics. The hope, or goal, was to gain a competitive advantage by marketing these animals directly to the packer.

If producers succeeded in doing this, then it was felt there would be **synergies throughout the entire value chain**.

The **key objective**—a truly important goal—was to maintain **independent, family-owned and operated farms** as the foundation and strategic advantage of the Ontario industry. We believed that land-based family operations delivered a huge advantage in many ways. They are proud producers: innovative, committed to quality, and tied to the land, which supports sustainability. Generally, community and family are important to these people. These were the values we aimed to preserve within the group we worked with. The plan: to help each participating individual meet their **business and personal goals**.

Of course, there were many steps required to bring this vision to life. The process didn't come without its challenges:

The University of Guelph (Dr. Kees DeLange) assisted with trials to establish two or three top genetic options and to develop nutrition programs tailored to them.

- Ultimately, NPD Genetics (now Hypor) became the genetic supplier for the system, with substantial guidance from Bob Fraser. We established a multiplier to kick off the process and set about implementing the plan.
- We decided to use a **three-site production system**.
- Discussions were held with candidate producers and potential investors to find the right fit. Would they just invest? Would they build or modify facilities? Would they take part in another link in the value chain? Slowly, the project took shape. Facilities were built, and the process began.
- We set health criteria and supported producers in transitioning their herds to a status that would fit the system. The focus was not just on achieving "good" health but on **stability and predictability**. Maintaining—or restoring—health status was, and remains, vital. This work started with my veterinary practice and eventually expanded to include Drs. Greg Wideman and Kevin Vilaca.
- Building a **sustainable pricing model** for pigs at production transition points (weanlings, feeders) was

another vital piece. Mark Yungblut took the lead here. Pricing between phases had to be fair for both buyer and seller—even if that meant no one was thrilled with the overall price. Without equitable pricing, the system would fall apart.

In 1999, it was decided to establish **Synergy Services**, a stand-alone business with separate shareholders, to manage the operations side of the Synergy system. This came in response to independent producers who wanted to participate in the system—whether by buying pigs, marketing collectively, or supplying stock.

Today, **Synergy Services manages "the pig"**—on behalf of various pig owners, including independent producers and companies. Management includes procurement, nutrition planning, health, production space management, record keeping, logistics, and marketing. Services are delivered on a **fee-per-pig basis**, not buried in other input costs.

This is a **vertically coordinated production system**. The model allows producers to own pigs at various stages of the system. For example, one might operate a sow herd and raise weanlings for the system while also owning finishing pigs—possibly in barns managed under contract by Synergy Services. Numerous ownership structures are possible. A young producer might start as a contract grower or rent a barn from a retiring farmer. Over time, they might transition into full ownership within the system. The same approach has been applied to sow barn ownership. These pathways have enabled **succession planning** and **next-generation entry** into the business. Several young farmers have grown into full operations this way.

Synergy Services exists to **raise the potential of people and pigs**. We strive to provide top-level management and marketing services to our clients—corporate and independent pork producers alike. Services field staff work directly with producers on-farm to ensure production stays on track. They also serve as key relationship holders with individual farmers. Similarly, our internal team manages all aspects of farm operations—from recordkeeping to complete management planning.

Our aim is to help members of the **Synergy family** meet their business and personal goals and to help their operations remain competitive. At the same time, we ensure their pork remains the product of choice for meat packers and their customers.

We also recognise that we have a responsibility—to our clients, their customers, and to the general public—to operate sustainably, produce safe and wholesome food, and uphold the humane treatment of animals.

As the business grew, the **vet practice grew alongside it**—a true synergy. Simultaneously, other swine practices across Ontario were evolving. Like their clients, these practices were trying to be all things to all people.

In 2010, after a few years of informal collaboration, **five Ontario vet practices** made the leap to amalgamate and form **Southwest Ontario Veterinary Services**—SW Vets. Given the strong personalities in each practice, it wasn't an easy path—but it was the right one. SW has grown into a team that serves the industry better than any of us could have done alone. That's what matters most.

This larger practice has enabled individuals to deepen their expertise in specific areas. The support team behind it has done meaningful work for the industry. Ontario has benefited from strong collaboration throughout the industry, especially through initiatives like the **Ontario Pork Industry Council**. In the health field, leadership from veterinarians such as **Drs. Doug MacDougald and Marty Misener** have brought the industry together to tackle health challenges.

This career has been fun. This industry has **fascinating people** and **ever-evolving challenges**.

What made it work?

For me, it was about being **“all in” every day**—committed, enthusiastic, and willing to do what it takes. The real joy is seeing others succeed—whether it’s producers, staff, or allies—as they grow along their own chosen paths.

It’s also deeply fulfilling to share a collective vision and work together as a community.

Chapter 10: Observations on Leadership

Dr. Bill Christianson

Bill retired as President of Genus PLC and PIC, Inc. Bill was the first person to prove it possible to eliminate the PRRS virus in a large system through medicated early weaning when he spearheaded the successful clean-up of the PIC breeding stock herds. He is very well known throughout Agriculture.

Observations on Leadership

William Christianson

When Ben contacted me about writing a chapter for this book, I was first honored, and secondly intrigued because many times in my career, I observed the "wasting" of experience when people retire. Of course, that doesn't mean accepting that experience is the only guide to the future or that you need to agree with everyone who has come before—it just means to me that it is valuable to consider the lessons people learn over a long career. I suppose another way to look at it would be to prevent the repetition of mistakes!

And speaking of a career, my introduction follows:

I grew up in an ag-based family in a small town in west-central Minnesota. One of 10 children (9 boys—we would have made a good boar multiplier), the family had a huge influence on me. I had overachieving siblings, so it was natural to scrap to get ahead myself. Integrity was drilled into us from little on, and so was the idea that you worked hard for things in life.

Academically, I went to St. John's in Minnesota (as did my brothers) and then to the University of Minnesota for veterinary school. After finishing vet school, I stayed on (partially based on Al Leman's advice—more about him later) for a PhD. My work centered on "Mystery Swine Disease," as it was known then. By the time I finished, we knew it as PRRS. At the time of my PhD work, there were about 10 faculty and 30 graduate students investigating all things pig-related in the "Swine Group." It was a fantastic time to be a student. My PhD advisor was Han Soo Joo, and I learned a lot from him—not least about Korea. I also met my future wife, Lucina, who was in Minnesota studying with Carlos Pijoan. We published a paper together on the interaction of PRRSv and Strep. Suis—now that's romantic.

As I finished vet school and then as a graduate student, I had the privilege to get to know Al Leman. He was just leaving the University of Minnesota, having built a world-class swine group from humble beginnings. He was transitioning to full-time at Swine Graphics, the commercial Iowa group started with Gene Barrick. Al took the time to mentor me on the side and had a huge influence on my development.

Sometimes, you just get lucky to meet the right people along the way. Sadly, he died at age 48 in 1992. I'll finish my intro on Al with a quote from the acknowledgments section of my PhD thesis: *I will always be thankful for knowing Al Leman. Al taught me about pigs and about life. His accomplishments were worthy of several lifetimes, but perhaps his uncanny ability to inspire those around him to solve problems, act on ideas, and strive to better themselves will be his greatest legacy.*

Following my PhD, I went to work for the Pig Improvement Company (PIC), starting as a research scientist on the veterinary side of things. PIC at that time was in transition from the entrepreneurial founder (Ken Woolley) to a large international professional company led by Phil David. I went to work for Maurice Bichard, the original technical director of PIC. I always felt lucky to have been able to meet and interact with those who were present at the beginning of PIC and to be part of the tremendous growth the company went through in subsequent years. My role in PIC evolved—after about a year and a half, by mutual consent, I moved into operations.

Over the following 30 years, I did many jobs in PIC—from vet services to genetics and production, sales, and general management of North America, and for the last 10 years of my career, I was the Chief Operating Officer for PIC globally. Along the way, I met and worked with countless individuals who helped me learn—and in doing so, I tried to be true to the "Never Stop Improving" mindset of the company. I retired in 2023 and left PIC in the capable hands of Matt Culbertson (jumping ahead a bit—I think you always want to leave things in hands more capable than your own!).

The format for my observations on leadership will be to use a quote, idea, or proverb (I read a lot) to make a point about leadership. The quote will be followed by a short description of how I think it applies. I did not list these thoughts in any order, and certainly, they are based on my opinions.

Expect much, give more. This one comes from Al Leman—in fact, it is part of a bullet list on his headstone in Webster City, Iowa. It took me a while to understand what he meant, but I think it is a key to effective leadership and tremendously powerful. The first part, *expect much*, was a constant reminder to me to expect a lot of others. In my experience, this is relatively rare—perhaps because people have been let down, perhaps because it is simply human nature—but it is amazing what people are capable of if you expect a lot of them. It also shows genuine confidence in people, and that inspires them. Plus, people do not want to disappoint. The second part, *give more* to me, really has to do with effective delegation. If you expect a lot of people, you need to support them in the right way—making sure they have the skills/tools to succeed. It also relates to setting good examples for those around you and helps solidify a feeling of team.

Fire in the belly is vital. Call it determination, drive, persistence, resilience, and stick-to-it-ness. This trait goes a long way to predicting success, in my experience. I once told my HR lead that if he could ever come up with a test that measured fire in the belly, it would be worth its weight in gold. Sadly, I'm not aware of such a test, and I think it fits into the 'you know it when you see it' category. Attracting and working with people who have this trait is a key part of success, I think – and it's fun!

Just keep in mind: the more we value things outside our control, the less control we have. This is a quote from Epictetus, the Roman stoic philosopher. It was a constant reminder to me to work on things we could control and not to waste time on things we couldn't. That is important for peace of mind and for a business to succeed.

People like to be around pleasant people. I once attended the Harvard Ag Seminar (a practice started in PIC by Ken Woolley) and in preparation, one of the suggested books to read was *How to Win Friends and Influence People* by Dale Carnegie. It was written during the Great Depression. It's amazing that it hasn't been topped in 90 years! Clearly, the pleasantness must be sincere, but it is a gentle reminder of a basic truth.

Trust is more important than being right all the time. A UK pig farmer told me this one day, and it stuck with me. Many things we do every day in a business build trust (and, of course, one mistake can destroy it; conversely, fixing mistakes builds trust). As technically trained individuals, I think it was important to realize you didn't have to be right all the time—an impossibility, really.

Don't try to be all things to all people, and saying no is often more important than saying yes. As humans, we want to please everyone, but oftentimes, that's just not possible, and it takes real discipline to say no. I found this to be particularly true in business. We had to define what we were good at and stick to that to grow—while coming up with alternate ways to meet market needs that weren't in our wheelhouse.

Things are rarely as bad or as good as they first appear. I don't remember exactly where I picked this up, but I found it to be true—in both directions. The English have their "Keep calm and carry on" from the war, and Lincoln used to say, "This too shall pass," both related to this point. It also relates back to the quote about working on things we can control.

Repetition works repeatedly. A simple, clear message repeated routinely helps build unity of purpose within an organization. At PIC, we developed a simple flywheel to describe what we did as a business. Everyone in the organization could speak to the flywheel and knew where and how they had an impact. That is but one example—there were many others over the years. As a leader, it may get old saying the same thing multiple times—but it is effective.

Quality trumps quantity regarding people, and good people don't like to sit on the bench. The first part is a quote from

Matt Culbertson, which is what we tried to live by at PIC—a sort of special forces approach. The second relates to many people's reviews where we would look at "bench" strength, and it dawned on me that the best wasn't satisfied being a backup on the bench. We had to challenge them. This is not an excuse to skip succession planning but rather a call to be creative in how you do it.

As a leader, you need to glance back occasionally to see if anyone is following you. I used this with a regional lead in the company who was excellent at charging ahead and taking on new initiatives. Unfortunately, I also had to remind myself to do this occasionally when some of my ideas failed to get traction.

The one who dares wins. Be bold. The first is the SAS motto that appears on Ken Woolley's footstone; the second is something Al Leman used to urge people (especially young people) to do. Different situations may call for a more careful or conservative approach, but Ken set out the entrepreneurial culture of PIC, which was something we guarded and tried to build upon. I suppose it relates in part to an attitude towards failure. We didn't want to make the same mistake repeatedly, but taking no risk wasn't an option in our business. Be bold—my example here was Al putting me in front to give a talk to hundreds of pig veterinarians when I had no business doing so. Like most people, I feared public speaking. I just needed to be bold and jump in—something Al could see. Another quote that fits here is from Shakespeare: "Our doubts are traitors and make us lose the good we oft might win, by fearing to attempt."

Confidence and arrogance can be close cousins. There is a fine line between being confident for all the right reasons and bragging or being arrogant, which has no place in business. I was constantly on the lookout for arrogance in the company and tried to stamp it out whenever I could. Far better to be humble.

Surround yourself with people who are better than you. I suppose this takes self-confidence, but in fact, it is critical. Great teams are made up of great people who all bring different skills or strengths to the table. Over the years, I observed managers who always needed to be the smartest person in the room, which usually meant the team wasn't that good. You need lots of smart people in the room. As a leader, I think one of your most important jobs is making sure your organization has great people. I also found that autonomy can be a significant motivator (it certainly was for me). To be able to truly give autonomy, you need good and capable people.

Honor the pioneers, but don't expect them to guide the future. I think it says a lot about company culture when people are genuinely proud of those who came before. However, guarding against "this is how we've always done it" is important for a leader. A thoughtful moment remembering the kind of leaders those pioneers were should help us realize we need to help forge the way forward in our own way.

Give other people credit. The rewards will be multi-fold. Whether it be citing foundational work that came before you, a contribution by a colleague, or from someone who works for you, giving people credit when it is due is the right thing to do and powerful. It also makes you a bit more pleasant.

Learning to listen can be hard work. I know it was (is) for me. It is also extremely important. Giving total attention to someone speaking is not natural for many of us—we race ahead and try to finish our thoughts, etc. By taking the time to truly listen, we learn.

If everyone agrees, then you don't really need a meeting. Modern life seems to be plagued by endless meetings. I think we need to be deliberate in calling for and attending appropriate meetings. I always encouraged healthy debate in meetings—sometimes heated discussion, but if there was mutual respect, it didn't carry over after the session and was useful. For me, it seemed a way to get to better decisions. I also liked to use the Socratic method of steering a discussion using questions—it was a great way to get people on board.

The process should make things easier or better; if it doesn't, ask why. In any large organization, a certain amount of process is inevitable and quite often critical. There is, however, based on my experience, a tendency for the process to become its own end. As I used to say to my young son regarding his math homework, make sure it makes sense.

We know more now. This comes from yet another Leman story. He gave a talk to a group of veterinarians, and one of the first questions from the audience was: "Al, you gave us a talk about the same subject a couple of years ago and told us something totally different. What gives?" He paused and then answered: "We know more now." In fact, I've found it is often difficult for people to change their minds on many things. Those that can, when presented with new information, are valuable. Another quote from Epictetus puts this in a different way: "It is impossible for a person to begin to learn what he thinks he already knows."

There is beauty in simplicity. I'm not sure where this came from, but I like it. I think we have a normal tendency to overcomplicate things, and usually, simpler is better. This can carry over into many aspects of business and life. Steve Jobs and others built businesses around this philosophy.

The cucumber is bitter? Then, throw it out. There are brambles in the path? Then go around. That is all you need to know.

—Marcus Aurelius, Roman emperor and stoic philosopher

Things happen. You've just got to deal with them and keep going forward. This is a favorite quote of mine because it is so practical and boils down a lot of truth into a few words. It is complemented by a quote from Hannibal, the great Carthaginian general: *You must find a way or make one.* This is from a guy who brought elephants via the Alps to invade Italy. Do you think you have challenges?

Now for some more historical quotes with short explanations if needed:

Nothing will ever be attempted if all possible objections must first be overcome.

This is a self-explanatory quote from Chinn Ho, a prominent businessman. I suppose this fits into the "be bold" theme from earlier. There are invariably reasons *not* to do things—these need to be weighed against all the positive reasons *to* do something.

The temptation to quit will be greatest just before you are about to succeed.

—A Chinese proverb.

I lived through this more than once and can attest to its wisdom. I think this applies particularly to entrepreneurial pursuits. For example, investing in a new approach or market often looks like a failure before it becomes a success. The trick, of course, is differentiating between things that may yet succeed and lost causes.

If you believe everything you read, better not read.

—Japanese proverb.

Again, self-explanatory. Be sure of your sources of information—and it generally helps to have more than one. This is especially true today, given the internet. We need to be thoughtful in how we accumulate information to make good decisions.

Men believe in the truth of all that is seen to be strongly believed in.

—German philosopher Nietzsche.

I think I've observed this phenomenon many times, and in fact, it can be a bit scary. There are salespeople who fit into this category. When it is based on truth, it can be powerful.

Things that matter most should never be put at risk by those that matter least.

—Sun Tzu.

He was, of course, referring to war, but it is equally true in business. I remember spending way too long on some internal company issues with my manager once and, in doing so, making us an hour late to a dinner with a customer whose business was larger than the entire market our internal discussions were focused on.

Every saint has a past, and every sinner has a future.

—Oscar Wilde.

This quote reminds us to use caution when judging people. Second chances, for the right reasons, can be transformative.

The dogs bark, but the caravan goes on.

—Arab proverb.

Again, things will happen, but life goes on—and as leaders, we need to help steer the ship through rocky waters. Our roles are partly about keeping the big picture in mind rather than the distractions of daily life.

I fear our mistakes more than the enemy's schemes.

—Athenian general Pericles.

We often get hung up on what competitors are doing rather than concentrating on how we can become better ourselves. We must understand and respect competitors but also find our own way and make sure we are doing what we set out to do well.

Not all those who wander are lost.

—J.R.R. Tolkien.

The business I was in had its share of characters and seemingly strange ways of doing things, but this was a reminder to me that you should take time to think—and that there are many paths to an answer.

I'd like to finish with two quotes from Napoleon because I think they are both big pictures, and they remind us that leadership can be used for good or bad.

A leader is a dealer in hope.

Everyone needs and wants hope in what they're doing, and like it or not, they often look to the leader to provide that hope. It is a big responsibility, but also an area where you, as a leader, can make a real difference. I think most people would like to be part of something bigger than themselves. The vision, the culture, the results—and yes, the hope—are all part of creating something bigger than ourselves.

Imagination rules the world.

Enough said.

Chapter 11: A chat with Dickson

Dickson Gould

Dickson is the Principal Owner and President of the Progressive Group of Companies. He also built and sold Elite Swine to Maple Leaf. He has been a force in the Pig Industry in Canada for many years.

I had the opportunity to sit down and interview Dickson for this book.

—Ben

A Chat with Dickson Gould

Dickson: Hey, how are you doing?

Ben: I'm doing great. How are you?

Dickson: Good.

Ben: Did you have a good time in Hawaii?

Dickson: Yeah, it was. It was. It was wonderful. Yeah, yeah.

Ben: Whereabouts were you?

Dickson: In Kauai and also like Honolulu, Waikiki, you know, as well as Pearl Harbour. It was pretty interesting.

Ben: You go there quite often?

Dickson: It's the first time I've ever been there.

Ben: OK.

Dickson: Yeah. We actually went with Greg Brown and his wife, so we had a good time.

Ben: Some interesting conversations with Greg, I'm sure.

Dickson: Oh, yeah, yeah, yeah. It was good.

Ben: Thanks very much for joining me for doing this, Dickson. Really appreciate it.

Dickson: Yeah.

Ben: I thought maybe it should be more of a conversation rather than an interview.

Dickson: Sure. That sounds good as well. I just reviewed the questions here, you know, just this morning again, so you ask, and I'll answer it as best as I can.

Ben: So maybe to start with, maybe you could just go through your journey because it'll act as a bit of a launching pad. Go through from the time you left school and your background and journey and how you got to where you're at now if that works.

Dickson: Yeah, sure. You know, I guess I took the extended program at university; I was playing hockey and different things. So I wasn't one of the guys that finished up in four years. I took the extended program and graduated, I guess, in the spring of '83 with a degree in Agri Economics.

Ben: You were on the same track as I. I played rugby at Georgia and it took an extra semester to get through as well.

Dickson: Yeah, yeah. Mine took a couple of years until I decided that I wasn't going to get drafted, so I better get at it.

Ben: Is that from the University of Manitoba?

Dickson: Yeah. I graduated—that was a very difficult time to actually get jobs. That was like during the depression there in the early '80s. So, I wanted to get on, and I enjoyed agriculture. My dad had farmed and then actually became a doctor later on. All my early years as a kid were spent on the farm, driving back and forth between Winnipeg and his farm. That was how I got involved in Ag, and that would be where my primary experience was as a child. I spent a lot of time milking and helping on my uncle's dairy farm.

So when I graduated, I thought there were some sales jobs in agriculture. I applied at many locations and sent resumes out everywhere. I got a chance with Bruce Campbell at Landmark Feeds and it was more of a connection at that time because our families knew each other. I got a chance to work there in October 1983 and it was kind of interesting— the way I got on was actually through a government program for university students. On a funny note, as I always told Bruce, I probably worked the first eight to nine months free because the program covered all of it.

It really wasn't a big risk for him, and I came in and worked at Landmark Feeds at the original feed mill in Landmark Manitoba. and basically, for the first four or five months, I worked in the feed mill making feed. Pulling the manual levers to make a batch of feed on a 2-ton batch Then, I got an opportunity to work the front desk and take the feed orders and make payments…interact with customers, and do poultry close-outs by hand. So that was my first experience.

There was another young guy named Rick Prejet, who had taken the diploma program at U of Manitoba and he was working at our sister mill doing dairy sales. Since I had a little experience on the dairy side, I spent time traveling with him and doing dairy sales in southeastern Manitoba; I was really kind of getting groomed to take on dairy sales.

They also fed some hog operations and really nobody put their hand up to do hog feed sales. So I said I had worked with hogs a little bit. Fortunately, they didn't ask what my experience was because we would run sows in a slough and put up snow fences to keep them in. This is how I got started working with the hogs.

We were in the very early stages of a little program called Elite Feeders. Ed Waddell started this program with a guy named Mark Milne. We were picking up weanlings from several small operations. The smallest were 100 sows, and the largest operation was around 240 sows owned by the Vielfaure family: Claude, Paul, Denis—father and uncle. We were mixing them all together from many different sources, in a 500-head barn. But that's the way everybody did it in those days. When they were short pigs, they went to the auction mart to get a load of feeder pigs. It was a little bit of the Wild West back then as far as health status. During that time we worked with Dr. Mike Sheridan, who was one of the leading vets on the swine production in Western Canada, and then worked with Dr. Paul Schneider who joined the same veterinary practice.

Ben: Yes, I know Mike and Doug MacDougald.

Dickson: Yes, he came on later. With the guidance of Mike Sheridan, we started to take a look at our pigs and saw we had different problems and different health statuses; so we started to do blood work and try to find out which ones could mix together. That was sort of the start of us really starting to understand the health status of the pigs we were buying. Also, during that time, we were also getting into newer types of genetics. The genetics on farms were all over the board from Cargill-type genetics to purebred breeders selling their genetics. Then one of the new companies, called PIC, was starting to sell genetics in our area focusing on increased genetic improvement. Feeding these new genetics, there were just a lot of challenges on nutrition and health status to get the higher lean indexes when the hogs were sold.

This was a really good time for a young guy to learn the business and to understand the basics of animal husbandry and the opportunity to learn all the things that we know today. Nobody gets that chance to be a generalist now—principles of nutrition, principles of ventilation, principles of disease/health status—and dealing with all these things all at the same time. Every day was a new adventure, and you learned how to sink or swim by your problem-solving skills, and never be scared to ask for advice to solve a problem.

Ben: Yeah.

Dickson: So, I learned ventilation rates from the early work that came out of VIDO on ventilation and what the minimum requirements are and everything like that. So, I really took it upon myself to learn the industry and go forward from there. So that worked. We did that in the early 90s. Then probably in the late 1990s, or right around there, we just said, hey, this is getting to be a bigger side of our business. To be successful going forward, we really have got to focus on it, and we've got to become better at it. This happens when you have competition. And we had a lot of good competition locally. We had the Puratone Corporation in Manitoba, which was growing their business. (Today, our present operations are housed in their office in Niverville, MB). They were fairly major competitors in our marketplace, and they were doing some interesting things there as well, too. What I am trying to say is that there was a lot of competition in our area. I think that's always healthy. I like the challenges of competition. I think the challenge of competition actually lifts up everybody's boats.

Ben: Right.

Dickson: We started to standardize barns and started to standardize genetics. We went a different path than others. We went with NPD Genetics at that time. We actually got a license to be a dealer in the province of Manitoba. We started to roll that side of the business. So, we wanted our herds all in the same health status. Then the right sire lines to it to bring standardization of our genetic program. In the mid-90s, we wanted to grow and expand the hog side of our business. The question was: "How should we do it?" The great thing was, Bruce Campbell really gave me the opportunity on the hog side to be in charge of Elite Swine Inc., where I was running that company at a young age. I learned a lot about managing people from trial and error on different things. I think one thing is that you run across people who really can make a big difference in your life and really take you under their wing and provide mentorship. They help you because they see that desire, that you want to learn and you want to get ahead, and people get attracted to that.

I was very fortunate to have those experiences, and mentor number one for me was obviously Bruce Campbell—and I'll talk about that later. There was one thing that was really interesting. You come back and you take a look at when big things happen, whether the events are positive or negative, there's always opportunities. One interesting event, and you would never think it would have impact on a little company in Manitoba, but it was when Joe Luter from Smithfield Foods bought the NPD Genetics franchise for the USA. In our minds, when he bought NPD Genetics, we just thought there could be an opportunity here for us, and maybe we could talk to him and his team. Maybe there's something that we can do. There was a sales guy who used to work for PIC, and now he works for NPD. He is named Jeremy Smith.

Ben: Yes, I know Jeremy.

Dickson: Jeremy was our NPD sales rep and he was also part of the responsibility of making sure things go smoothly here and in the U.S. for NPD. In short order, Jeremy, upon our request, lined up a meeting with Smithfield—with Joe Luter, Greg Schmidt, and Bo Manley. We also had a meeting with them at their corporate head office in Smithfield, Virginia. We had roughly 10,000 to 15,000 sows back then, and we talked to them about our health being very good and stable. We asked if there were any opportunities for us to stock some barns with F2 gilts (F1 gilts backcrossed with Large White semen) for them and help them with their expansion plans. I still remember that meeting vividly. Prior to going, I said, "Where are we meeting? Is that in North Carolina, or is that Virginia? Where should we fly to?" None of us had ever been to North Carolina or Virginia. I remember Bruce coming downstairs one day and saying, “Who has these expensive phone calls to Warsaw, Poland?” All he could see were calls going to

Warsaw—which was actually in North Carolina! So, he was wondering what was going on. Anyway, we met with them.

With Joe Luter—I had never seen guys who talked like that. He asked Greg and Bo how the expansion plans were coming along. They said they were going well, and he said, "Well, can we double them?" Then he just put his hands on the table, and these guys went pale white! And, you know, there was just me, Ed Waddell, Dr. Paul Schneider, and Gary Stott. We just said, "Holy mackerel, this is a different league than what we're in!"

Anyway, when we came out of that meeting, we said maybe this is something that can work with Browns of Carolina. Boy, oh boy! So we and Joe Luter assisted us with an opportunity to maybe do something with the Browns of Carolina. We ended up putting a deal together, and we probably exported close to 30,000 to 40,000 gilts to them over a four- or five-year period.

We saw what they were doing in North Carolina. They were commissioning a barn a day—five barns a week—and they were putting up one or two finishing barns a week. What we saw there was that if you want to do something, you've got to standardize, and you've got to have standardization.

So, we came back and said that one of the key learnings is standardization. To put barns together and have the same equipment, ventilation, and barn size. Historically, our guys would say, “I only have enough money for 600 sows,” and then another might have 800.

We thought we didn't have to necessarily move to North Carolina to do that. Can't we do it in Manitoba? So that's how that all came about.

That year, we developed a business plan and standardized the size of the barns at 2,850 sows, and that's how we got to 2,000 head finishing barns for one week’s production coming from two sites, with 500 smaller pigs going to an overflow barn. This became our business model based on standardization. This was a really good experience. By doing this deal in North Carolina it was more than a gilt deal—it was the mentoring and getting exposure to new ideas. Seeing what equipment people were using and the contacts that we gained really helped to crystallize our vision.

Greg Brown became a really good mentor and a really good person to talk to because he started up stuff on his own and how he dealt with certain situations and transitions. And that was really valuable. Very valuable.

Ben: OK. And so when you say you expanded in Manitoba, that was commercial production, presumably?

Dickson: Yeah, that was a commercial production business in Manitoba. Between that time and 1999, Maple Leaf was looking at building a processing plant. We were shipping market hogs to them in Burlington, Ontario, at the Fearman's plant. They asked us our opinion on where to locate the plant, and we suggested the Westman region. They decided that Brandon would be the ideal location, and so they built a plant. But had no hogs.

Ben: Right.

Dickson: Within our ownership group, there were some junior owners like me. But for the senior guys, this really became a pretty nice exit strategy for them. So, in October of 1999, we sold the business to Maple Leaf. That worked out well for Maple Leaf, and that also worked out well for our ownership group. For me, it worked out well, too, because I had the opportunity to work in a publicly traded company on their executive team.

Ben: So you worked at Maple Leaf?

Dickson: Yeah, yeah. I ran the Elite Swine program, and they wanted us to grow some more.

Ben: OK.

Dickson: We grew our footprint from Manitoba. ESI had 25,000 sows in Alberta, and we had 70,000 sows in Manitoba. We also had some fairly major expansion in Eastern Canada through the Shur-Gain side. When I left, we had 103,000 sows on the program with a great team... Brock Campbell, Howard Siemens,

David Penner, Guy Baudry, Dr. Paul Schneider, Don Downs, Scott Dick… all leaders in the Canadian swine industry.

Ben: Oh yeah, yeah.

Dickson: That was a really interesting period of time because I got a chance. One person I met there who was really just the salt of the earth was Wallace McCain, and Wallace was just an exceptional person. He knew what it was like to start something from scratch, and we had a lot of great conversations. That is probably what I cherish the most. One of my cherished things was the day I left—he wrote me a nice letter. And I still have that to this day. It was really, really nice.

I had the opportunity there where I had the two-year non-compete, and even with that two-year non-compete, I actually stayed on four years because I just really enjoyed it. I got to learn about publicly traded companies. I got to learn about the finance side of the business a little bit better, and budgeting, and the importance of budgeting for bigger companies—and how public companies think and focus. There's a lot you learn when you work for a good, successful entrepreneurial company. Then, you go to a publicly traded company and learn a lot about what makes them work.

If there's a gap in learning, and "you know what you don't know," you can learn a lot and be a sponge. To be successful, you have to influence people if you want to get stuff done!

That was a great time. Those years included a lot of nights where you're working day and night, but it was really fun. We had a program where we brought in a lot of young, talented people into our company. For example, we brought people in like Guy Baudry, who was our RBC banker out in Brandon. He had roots in Eastern Manitoba, and we just said to him, "Maybe this will be a little bit more exciting than banking. We are growing our brand and operation."

So, I was driving back and forth between Landmark and Brandon, trying to develop that business in the Westman area. But if we wanted to be successful, we needed to actually have our own team out there. To do that, you've got to have a really good leader. Guy Baudry came in to run the West office, and we built an A-Team around him. Then Howard Siemens, who used to be a young guy going to high school— ran sows in a hip-roof barn. I did a little bit of feed business with this young guy. When he graduated from Grade 11, we said, "Why don't you come to work for us during the next summer, go to school, and then next summer, you know you've got a job with us." Howard came on side with us as well.

They were all really entrepreneurial men, always asking a lot of questions, and really wanted to understand things. Howard ended up running our whole production.

And then there was Dave Penner. He worked at a hog farm while he was going to university over by Sanford. He was working at Regal Feeds, and Dave was just a very button-down guy. He was always reading and writing. He worked on development—getting the barns and plans lined up—but he was really solid on production as well. He had really, really strong relationships.

When the Landmark group brought the Purina feed mill to Strathmore, Alberta, the feed business plan was based on having some hog business. This required Ed Waddell to move out West to lead that charge, and he did a great job in a challenging market.

Brent Moen took a leadership role, along with Gary Friesen, and so we had a really, really great team. It was a group of people that came up together, and they just worked very, very hard and were very, very dedicated. The vast majority of the team is still involved in advancing the hog industry to this day.

You can't grow your business if you don't have good people.

Trying to do everything yourself? You know you'll burn out. You might be good, but you'll never have the economies of scale if you can't get along with people and you can't work with people!

It is important to be able to communicate transparently. One thing that we've always had in our meetings was that if you disagree with something, let's talk about it. Let's be transparent about it. Not just kind of keep it inside. Things always come up, so let's talk about it—because no one person has all the answers.

Usually, it's a consortium of input by people that actually can give you the right answer, and it's whether or not it's the answer you would like to have. I always believe in a consortium of people working together and getting good people's input.

There's a role for the leader to separate out the chaff from the wheat. But it's good to have input and to holistically look at it and say, "Will this work?" Hog production is like a balloon—you push your finger in somewhere, thinking that you're going to save something, but it bubbles out somewhere else. You've got to understand all the dynamics and think those things through.

Paul Schneider came on board with us very early, in the 90s. He did a wonderful job as a veterinarian. His guidance really helped us to ensure that our health status stayed consistent.

Ben: It's so important.

Dickson: Oh, exactly. We had a great team of people in all aspects of the business, and I think part of that is also having a vision of what you want to accomplish—and how those people can be part of that vision—and that they can also see themselves as being part of that vision. It is really, really important. The economics have to work for people. But making sure that they really have a work ethic, desire to achieve, and a passion to make a difference—I think those are areas that are really important. And developing a structure to work with—they need to be able to see where they fit into that structure.

This was all Elite Swine, and it got incorporated into Maple Leaf. All these people were part of the Elite Swine Landmark Feeds group.

Ben: And so why did you wind up leaving Elite/Maple Leaf?

Dickson: It was primarily for two reasons. Number one is that we were in a publicly traded company. I was the president of the swine division. You have to remember when you're in a privately held company, you have opportunities to co-invest. You don't necessarily get those opportunities when you're in a publicly traded company.

I was signing contracts with myself—all above board, and they knew exactly what was going on—but I was also in that difficult situation.

The second reason was I had three sons at home. At that time, the oldest one would have been—this was in 2003—14 or 15 years old. And then I had two other boys. So I made a decision: if I ever wanted the opportunity to do something with my boys, then I probably needed to get at it because to grow a business takes 25 years. It just doesn't happen overnight.

There are some people—everything they touch turns to gold. But you know what I found is that there's a lot of years of patience that you have to deal with. And as you get older, it gets tougher and tougher to deal with those years of patience than when you're young.

I had investments in farms, and I dealt with everything on the Maple Leaf side during the week. My wife also did all the books for our businesses. Saturday and Sunday, I was signing checks and going through our farms. I just said to myself, I can do this for a period of time, but the bottom line is, if I want to do something, then I'd better make a change—retire from Maple Leaf—and just review and strategize about what we can do.

So I left in October 2003. That was exactly 20 years to the day from when I started.

I think it caught a lot of people off guard. But you know, at the end of the day, I wanted to go in a different direction. From my standpoint, I just figured that was a good time to go and see where it would take me.

I really enjoyed working for Scott McCain and Michael McCain. Michael always treated me well. Everybody treated me well there, so I had no ill will with Maple Leaf at all. I was probably 45 years old, and I figured if I was going to do something, that was the time. I had a window where I could do something else. And if I hadn't made that decision, I'd still be at Maple Leaf today.

Ben: So, then you left Maple Leaf, and that was—and you had a two-year agreement with them that you wouldn't get back into pigs again?

Dickson: Oh no, that was over because that was in 1999, and the non-compete had run out while I was still there. I'd been with them for four years, so that was no issue. Yeah.

Ben: Right. That was probably a pretty tough time because you were going through the late '90s, which was a pretty tough time in the industry as well.

Dickson: Oh yeah, yeah, it was. But through 1998—like 1998—we actually did fairly well. We weren't going to sell pigs at $50 a piece.

So, we figured out a strategy to basically park the pigs until the market turned around and we could get a higher price for them. We basically just fed dry sow diets to our whole system, waited out 3–4 weeks, and then started shipping hogs again. By then, they had gone up to $125.

We were fortunate to go through that, and we were also building barns so that we had some extra barns that we could move pigs into and stuff like that. We were very fortunate during that period of time. But we came through that one fairly well.

Ben: So then you left Maple Leaf and started Progressive?

Dickson: Yeah. In the fall of 2003. As I mentioned, my wife was doing the books for the farms, and so I started to get a little bit more involved in the farms—going down to the farms on a weekly basis and working with them. I also started networking a little bit to find out what was going to become available.

There was a lot of strife in the hog markets, and I figured it was a matter of time until there were going to be some assets coming up for sale.

Brock Campbell, my business partner since 1990—we became buyers of good-quality assets with our investment partners, but they weren't properly managed, or they got into some level of financial difficulty. We ended up buying quite a few units. We bought two sites from Premium Pork, and we bought some from another local company. We grew our business quite a bit by acquiring some depressed assets.

I managed the new sites, created payroll, and exported a lot of weanlings down south to the USA from 2003 to 2007.

Every time a kid went to university or left home, we converted another bedroom into an office. We had four or five people doing bookwork at our place and my wife in our office with a divider.

At some point, our neighbors would complain that they couldn't get down the street because there were too many cars on the street. That led us to a more professional approach.

That year, we secured an office in Niverville that was being used as a real estate office. It was a nice office—professional look—and the good news, or bad news, was the other half of the office was a Subway franchise. After I left there, I couldn't eat at Subway for four years. Just the smell of that bread was on my lips all the time.

That was in 2007 in the early spring. I said to Brock, who had been my partner since 1990, "Brock, this is getting too much, and I probably need your help." He left Maple Leaf in 2007, and we set up the company called the **Progressive Group of Companies Inc.**

The idea was that there was also an opportunity at that time because Maple Leaf didn't want to have partners anymore on their sow operations.

There was a lot of horse-trading of assets where we were in partnerships with them because they wanted to buy us out—and we really didn't want to sell. We were accumulators, not sellers.

We did a lot of horse trading, and we got a bunch of assets around the southeast corner of Manitoba, and they secured some assets around their Brandon plant.

Some of our original partners that we were involved with didn't want to sell, so we came in as partners with them and were able to acquire MLF's interest in these operations.

Some independent owners needed management services, payroll services, and veterinarian services—and they approached us about helping them out.

We took a look at all that and decided we could do it. That way, we could help out a few of our partners, but we were not going to go and put a shingle out saying that we would concentrate on contract management, swine production, or anything like that.

So, we worked with—and we still work with—the same partners to date that we worked with at the very beginning. We wanted to use that as a vehicle to grow our business and try to become good at it. This allowed us to get to a certain size where we could actually bring in a veterinarian on a consulting basis, and so we did that.

Then, we went through a very difficult time in Manitoba because there was a moratorium, and we couldn't grow or expand. This allowed us to diversify into two other businesses.

First of all, **Rainbow Trailers** is a trailer manufacturing business in Cartwright (southwest Manitoba). Then we got into **Winkler Meats**, which was another business— a federally inspected plant with some branded products in Winkler. We have stayed in those businesses and grown those businesses over the years.

Ben: I know that's a whole different ballgame—running a plant. The meat business versus the production business.

Dickson: Oh, yeah, yeah, yeah. You know, I can say we definitely had a college education in the learning process!

Ben: It was a very steep learning curve for me, that's for sure.

Dickson: The trailer business was smoother because we inherited a really good business team that was very responsible. We basically just followed their lead, and that was very fortunate. We were really fortunate there!

But on the meat side, at Winkler, when we took over the meat business, it was doing everything. It was doing buffalo, elk, and even ostriches at that plant—and those people were able to make it go. Then, with BSE, what could we do with all the byproducts?

So we just said either we're going to go broke or we're going to have to come up with a solution. One of our philosophies is if something's not working, you either sell it or fix it.

We decided to fix it, and we made some structural changes to the business model. We decided we were just going to do one species and let everything else fall by the wayside. We weren't very popular with the buffalo people and the elk people, but they couldn't pay enough to make it work.

Ben: So then William, your son, came to work with you in the business. What about your other sons?

Dickson: William was a lawyer, and he worked downtown Winnipeg with one of the larger firms and did commercial law. We have family meetings every year, and we talk about things. I'd say to them, it's always important to me that you go out and work somewhere and get some experience. And if they really liked it, then they should stick with it.

I really wanted to make sure my family could be involved in our business, but I didn't want it to be a mission project. It cannot be a make-work or mission project. If you have a mission project, you can do that on your personal time, but not in a business where you've got other partners. I wanted to make sure people would contribute.

So, William came back after five years and said, "Hey, you know what? If you're open, I wouldn't mind coming on board." We sat down and talked about economics and everything, and fortunately, it worked out very, very well. I think that it's also important, in a family-run business where there's the Campbell and the Goulds family, that we have alignment. Brock was on the side as well, and it's worked out very well. I would say even better than expected.

William brought different skill sets that we didn't have, which I think is important. When you grow and do things, some areas become somewhat sacred cows, and he came back and challenged us. I think that was good for the business.

You know, for all of us, the industry changes and grows. There's a whole new generation of new people coming up in the industry, and it's really important for them to network. Opportunities like the leadership program that you developed— That course, and also the 21st Century Next Generation with the young guns— are really good networking opportunities for this next generation, and I think that's a really great service. It's also something that expands your horizons and allows you to get to know people.

Like Brock and I always say, if you don't get out and about and talk to people, you don't learn things. I think that's something that's very important.

You've got to make sure you get your job done, and there are day-to-day things that have to be done, but you've got to have the mindset to be open to new ideas. New ideas are not always coming from the industry; they could be coming from other businesses that can be adapted to your industry.

Ben: I really enjoyed getting to know William. He's very smart and thoughtful. He really brings a lot to our meetings as well. He's always got interesting questions for people and always thinks carefully. He looks at things in a different way than a lot of people.

And so your other two sons?

Dickson: Yeah. The other two sons. One is in New York now, and he works with Aetna, one of the insurance companies. He has a senior role there, and he's an actuary by trade. And it's kind of funny because Brock, my partner, his oldest guy, is graduating this year from U of M with an Actuarial degree.

Then, my youngest guy is working with Topigs/Norsvin. He is working with the data/AI side of the genetic business. He's starting to learn the business with Topigs on the genetics side.

All three boys worked on farms as they grew up, and those experiences have helped them.

Ben: And do you think it's likely that he'll come back at some point in time?

Dickson:

Yeah, he's learning the business from that standpoint. And you know, I think he's really getting into it and is developing a passion for it. We'll see where it goes because we're looking for people with passion. He's really strong in IT and artificial intelligence. This is becoming a bigger and bigger area of opportunity, which I know we have to understand.

We have to figure out artificial intelligence if we want to remain successful in the future. Brock and I are not necessarily sure that we are the right ones to figure this out. I kind of know what I'm looking for, but I don't know how to get there. But we are good at plagiarizing. The next generation has—and will be—providing that expertise.

Ben: You know, that's really something important.

Dickson: Yeah.

Ben: So, is there anything else as far as your journey goes that you think of?

Dickson: Well, I spend a lot of time now on boards and different things in the industry, trying to help out wherever I can.

But no, I think that gives you a little background on what I've done, yeah.

Ben: And so, as far as motivation and managing your employees, what do you think are the keys to that? You said that it was really important to build that team at Maple Leaf. How did you do that? What are the keys to keeping people motivated and happy, moving forward, and looking forward to coming to work? I've seen companies that really beat people down, and I’ve seen the opposite. Everybody has a different philosophy on that.

Dickson: I think the one thing is to have clarity on what you're trying to accomplish. That is what we're trying to do right now and really focus on—particularly when we talk on the pig side of the business—to focus on swine production excellence and performance excellence, and we are working on that.

So, you need to have a vision of what you want to be able to accomplish. Having a vision of how we want to grow our business. We do a little bit of expansion, but most of our expansion is taking existing sites and making them bigger rather than going out and buying things all over the place. We've been opportunistic, and we'll still be opportunistic when things come up. But really, what we want to make sure is that we've got our stuff close to home so that we can have economies of scale.

Here’s an example: in the group housing, we're really taking a look at taking some of our 3000 sow units and maybe taking them from 3000 to 5000, depending on our flow requirements. Whether we can be more efficient with our conversions and make our operations more efficient on our operational side, these are the areas that we're focusing on.

I think people having that vision and showing them how they can be part of the vision and how they can help to make a difference is really, really important.

One thing that came up that I remember was we had an HR person who came in back in the Maple Leaf days, and he said, you know—your oldest plumber or your most senior plumber may not be the best manager of the plumbing department, right? Make sure you identify and challenge your team to make sure that you have the right leaders.

As you grow your business, one thing that's really important is to try to educate the people and give them positive exposure and experiences so that, as you're growing and as they're taking on responsibility, they are capable of handling it. In a lot of situations, that works very well.

There are some people, unfortunately, that get tapped out. It's not always that they get tapped out, but that they get to a point where they feel entitlement—that they should get that next position—rather than actually earning it. And I think the better way to do it is by earning it.

Those are the areas where, as managers and owners, it's really important to give people the chance to move up. And give them the skill sets to take them to the next level. And it's really worked well for us as the sow manager.

Basically, we've got a lot of new technology. We've got a lot of change management. And it's really important to get them familiar with stuff well in advance so that when the technology changes come, or management changes happen, they're mentally prepared for both.

They've also got, in their minds, operationally, how they can work with the changes and what the benefits are. So that's really worked well for us.

It takes a little bit longer to do, but it's about bringing everybody on board, educating them, and bringing everybody up to the next level. I think that's really important.

I think the other thing that's really important is to take people's input and be a good listener. A lot of times, the best stuff comes right from the floor level. Whether it's the guy on the floor or a guy in the office—it doesn't matter where he or she is—everybody's got value that they can bring, and it's recognizing that value.

Letting them know that it's important really helps. Once you get that trust level with staff and people, and you're consistent all the time, there are a lot of good things that come out of that. Your people can help you with your recruiting.

Then, there are a lot of benefits that come with helping your people succeed. When I was overseeing farms, I told the farm manager: “My goal is to help you to make the biggest bonus possible for you and your team.” Then we're totally aligned.

Ben: And you talked about your mentors.

Dickson: Yeah, I like mentors—people that have been really helpful. Obviously, there was Bruce Campbell. I had the opportunity to work alongside Bruce for many years, and what always stuck in my mind was that there is really only one way to deal with things.

Problems are always going to happen if you are dealing with livestock or feed or whatever. There are always going to be issues. But you always deal with those issues by taking the high road. You treat people—such as customers or your partners—better than they would treat you. Our partners have treated us very, very well, but it is the concept of treating people better than yourself.

If you go in with that mindset, it's amazing what you can get accomplished. Then, when there are problems, they become long-term opportunities because people remember how you handle problems. That goes for a lot of decisions that happen both in business and at home. Then Bruce always wanted things to look professional. And he made sure, however, you do it, to make sure you are professional and make sure your staff are professional and you have a professional culture.

I went to meetings of other companies where everybody was swearing at a meeting. But we do it differently—and professionally—as we can, based on Christian principles. Those are things that we follow to this day, and we give people opportunities. Take a look at who you do business with, treat them fairly, and update them so that they want to do business with you again.

These values are so important—with the bankers and our partners—so that when problems happen, or bad market conditions or other things come up, you are actually ahead of it and proactively talking to everybody ahead of time.

One of our business principles, which is kind of interesting, is when we start a new venture or business, "let's not tax it" with any additional overhead or put pressure on it by taking money out of it that it can't afford. Let's put your money in and leave it there. We'll leave it there for five to seven years before we start taking any money out. That way, it's really well secured. Then, you are in a strong fiscal position. A lot of people don't want to do that. They think that everything's going to work out, everything's going to cash flow, and everything is going to be fine.

And sometimes those businesses come up for sale in a few years—even though they're a good business—because everything's been bled out of them.

We look at this as a long-run decision, and we want to support it and make it work.

Then generally, what we've done is—you know, when the opportunity comes to take money out of a business—we generally only take 50% of it, and we leave the other 50% in every year.

That way, the business has money to operate with, and it always allows it to deal from the point of strength.

That has worked out well for us and allows us to grow our business. And then, if we can take money out, we can reinvest it somewhere else. But generally, we keep it within that particular company to make sure it stays strong.

Ben: It has been an hour and fifteen minutes. I don't want to take up too much of your time. I really appreciate you doing this, Dickson. I know you have a deeply rooted Christian faith. Do you feel like faith plays a big part in your work, or do you try to keep that completely separate? How does that guide you?

Dickson: You know, I don't get involved in telling people what faith they should have or not. It's more important that they have a faith—one or another. It's kind of interesting for me because I was a Protestant boy going to a Jesuit school. And my children—some are Protestant, and some are Catholic—depending on the influence, and that's terrific.

But the one thing I learned from the Jesuit school that really stuck with me is that sometimes when you are problem-solving, and you're dealing with issues, it's really important to have a full understanding of what the issues actually are and what the problem is. If the solution is only that I win, I really haven't solved the problem. So, think of it from a from a bigger perspective, a holistic approach.

How does this work for my business and people, but equally importantly, how does it work for other people? How does it work for *you* and the individuals?

Also, if somebody is upset or something just doesn't make sense, there are usually some personal issues or problems that somebody has. That is really the source of the issue, and you cannot get offended by those things.

So take a deep breath and look at how we can help them with those other areas, as well as what the issue is. I think it's taking a wider look at how we do things.

I think, you know, one nice thing about being in agriculture is that we require good weather. We require a lot of things that are out of our control. And every once in a while, we have to give thanks for things when everything goes right—and not panic when things are wrong. Because, you know, we just have to work through them.

For a long time, Brock and I never took anything out of our business. Basically, we put everything back into it to grow the business. And there's a lot of people that don't do that. With that discipline and a desire to do that, we have been very fortunate. There are probably a lot easier ways to make money than what we do. But we enjoy what we do, and the people we work with—and that is priceless!

Another thing is that we have probably 20-plus partnerships, and we've never had a harsh word with any of our partners.

Ben: Do you ever get mad? I've never seen you mad.

Dickson: No, I don’t get mad. I just… you know, I just, I—I don't get too worked up.

Ben: I didn't think so. I've really enjoyed getting to know you over the years and working with you on different things. It's been a real pleasure working with you, and I've certainly learned a lot from you as well. You know, it's interesting hearing you talk about the Smithfield guys because, obviously, I knew Randy Stoecker very well.

Dickson: Yeah.

Ben: Wendell Murphy, as well. And so there are a lot of similar people with whom we have crossed paths.

Dickson: One thing you have in your questions is advice for young people starting out their career in the industry. Number one is to get as much experience as you can.

Being a learner—an active learner, a continuous learner—is really important.

Then, also, in a roundabout way, you find some mentors that you can work with that you know can help you, and you know you can feel like you can give them a call and ask them for their advice. And I think that's really important. There are lots of mentors, but you want to find the good ones.

Ben: And that's what Randy was to me after my dad died because my dad died when I was pretty young in my working life.

Dickson: OK. Does that help you out?

Ben: That is great. I really appreciate it.

It was really interesting talking to you and hearing about your journey, and I'm looking forward to putting all that together.

I'll send you a copy before I finalize it so you can read through it and make sure that there's nothing wrong.

Ben: Great to talk to you, Dickson. Bye.

Dickson: Yeah. Take care. Goodbye.

Chapter 12: Why leadership training is so important

Shonda Sammons

Shonda is my Business Partner in the 21st Century Leadership Forums. She is widely known for her ability to connect with young managers and help them flourish and grow. She is a brilliant Leadership Consultant and resides in Southern Kentucky.

The Value of Leadership Development Programs

By Shonda Sammons

Leadership development programs can drive both organizational and individual success. From an organizational perspective, the return on investment can be seen throughout all areas of the business. Financial performance improves as more capable leaders initiate productivity and efficiency within their teams. Collaboration is possible when leaders develop stronger relationships between departments by breaking down silos. The organization also sees substantial cost savings through reduced turnover because employees who see clear growth opportunities are more likely to build their careers internally rather than seeking advancement elsewhere.

The cultural impact runs deep within organizations that prioritize leadership development. As leaders establish their capabilities, they become more effective at communication. They realize the importance of communicating organizational values and connecting their teams to the broader mission and vision. This alignment creates a more cohesive workplace where employees understand how their work contributes to organizational goals.

For employees, the benefits of leadership development extend far beyond learning new skills. Participants gain increased confidence in their abilities and develop a stronger sense of purpose in their roles. They establish competencies in strategic thinking, problem-solving, and decision-making that enhance their influence and job fulfillment. The opportunity to grow professionally while remaining with their current organization creates a deep sense of loyalty.

The effects on employee engagement are particularly noteworthy. When employees see their organization investing in their development, it strengthens their emotional connection to the company and translates into a sense of belonging. This feeling of belonging is foundational to building trust within teams and the organization. A high level of trust makes it safe for employees to be more proactive in suggesting improvements, taking initiative, and holding each other accountable. This heightened engagement also translates into measurable improvements in team performance and innovation.

Commitment to their teams and the organization is also fostered through leadership development and can be expressed in several ways. Employees demonstrate greater flexibility during challenging times and show a willingness to go above and beyond to achieve organizational goals. Employees become more invested in the company's success and take ownership of their role in achieving it. This commitment spreads throughout the organization as developed leaders model these behaviours for their teams.

From a succession planning perspective, leadership development ensures organizational continuity by preparing the next generation of leaders. Rather than having to look externally to fill key positions, organizations can promote from within, maintaining cultural consistency and institutional knowledge. This creates a sustainable model for organizational growth while providing compelling career paths for ambitious employees, especially early-stage professionals.

The financial returns on leadership development extend beyond direct metrics. Engaged and committed employees are more productive and make fewer mistakes. They're more likely to identify and implement process improvements that save money or generate new revenue opportunities. The cumulative effect of these improvements significantly impacts the organization's bottom line.

Most importantly, strong leadership development programs create a learning environment that promotes adaptability and resilience. These skills are increasingly valuable in today's rapidly changing business environment, enabling organizations to respond effectively to new challenges and opportunities.

Epilogue

Not exactly your standard management or leadership book, is it?

Hopefully, you got some interesting nuggets from it. When I read a book, if I can get two or three takeaways, then it has been a worthwhile exercise.

My father built the largest pig breeding company in the world, PIC. Dr. Jan Schuiteman, a very well-respected veterinarian, businessman, and the founder of Trans Ova, once told me he thought my dad was a genius.

However, I've also had people tell me that when they came out of meetings with my dad, they sometimes had no idea what he wanted them to do—because he was talking about things five or ten years in the future.

In my observations, the most successful leaders set out and communicate the vision and then empower people to achieve those goals.

My mother used to say, "Get really smart people together and get out of the way." That was PIC, especially in the early days.

Surround yourself with good people and then try not to hamstring them with bureaucracy. Let them succeed, and reward them when they do.

Thank you again to all who contributed to this book. Their generosity of time is what made the book possible. I cannot tell them enough how grateful I am.

Good luck, and go get 'em!!

Made in the USA
Columbia, SC
12 July 2025

7d896fa2-7352-44e1-b596-09ae1e25f65aR01